Dot-to-Dot

FOR GROWN-UPS

Dot-to-Dot
FOR GROWN-UPS

Create Intriguing Visual Puzzles

DAVID WOODROFFE

ARCTURUS

ARCTURUS

This edition published in 2015 by Arcturus Publishing Limited
26/27 Bickels Yard, 151–153 Bermondsey Street,
London SE1 3HA

ISBN: 978-1-78212-940-0
AD004049NT

Printed in China

Contents

Introduction

Put two dots on a clean sheet of paper and inevitably someone will take a pencil and draw a line between them. So that's what we've done in this book, except that each page contains up to four hundred consecutively numbered dots waiting to be joined together by someone with a sharp eye and pencil. In a few cases, pictures are made from more than one continuous line. Look out for the notes identifying these.

Be prepared for a journey that will unlock famous works of art and scenes from the world of entertainment, sport, transport and the natural world. But don't expect an easy ride. Sometimes the next number may be difficult to find, but with patience, a pencil and a straight edge the final picture will be revealed! And if an image looks familiar but you just can't remember its name, you'll find the answer at the back of the book.

Before you begin in earnest, try your hand at the dot-to-dot below.

David Woodroffe

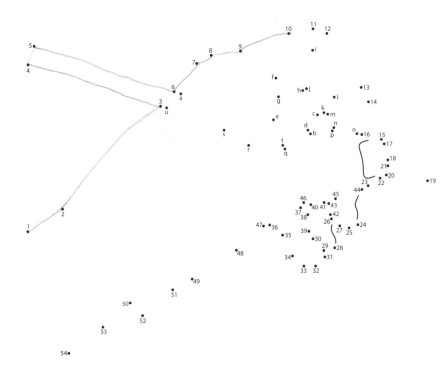

This picture is made from 2 continuous lines:
a) number and b) lower case letters

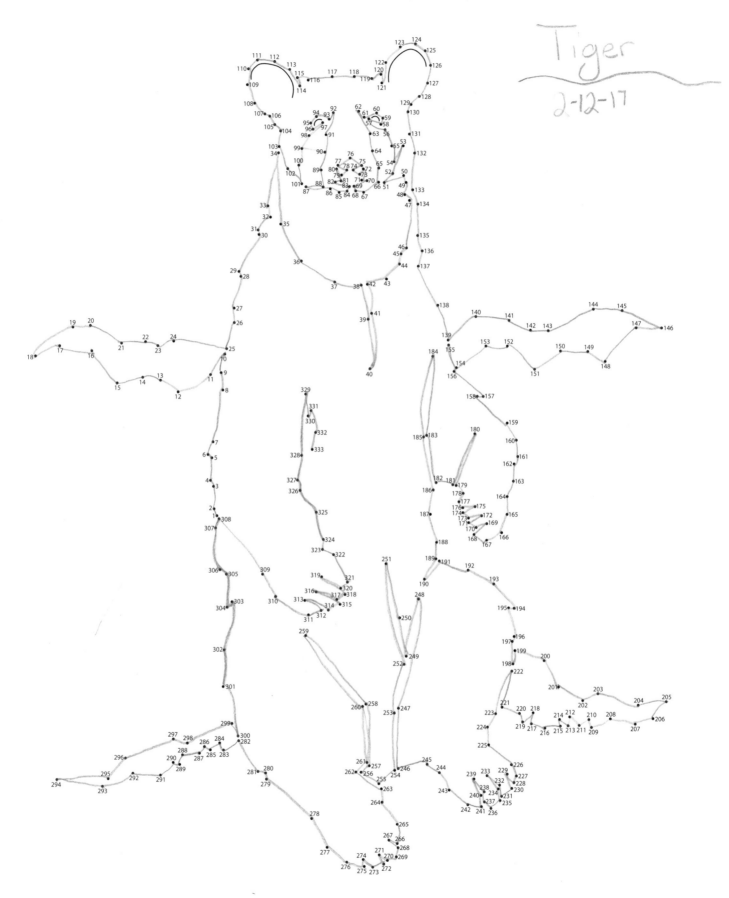

Tiger
2-12-17

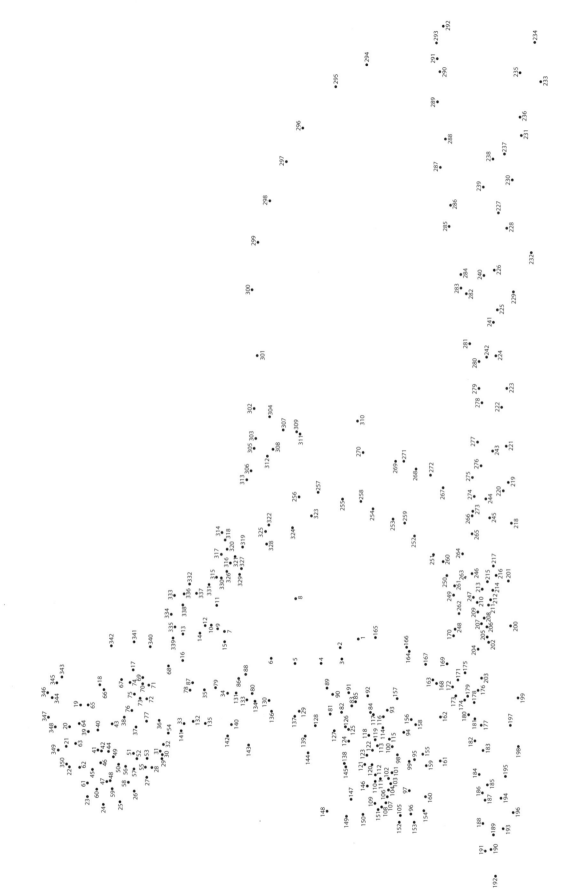

9

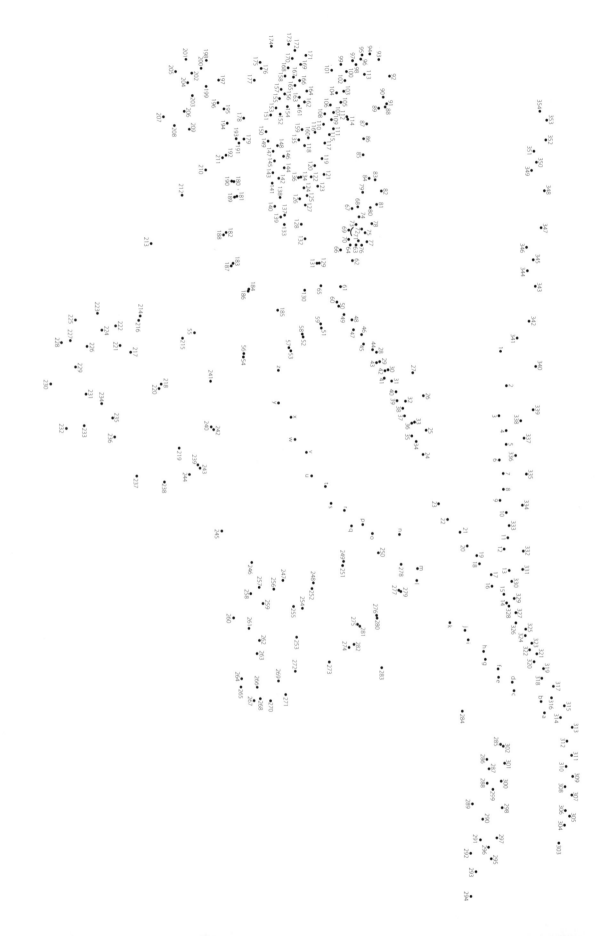

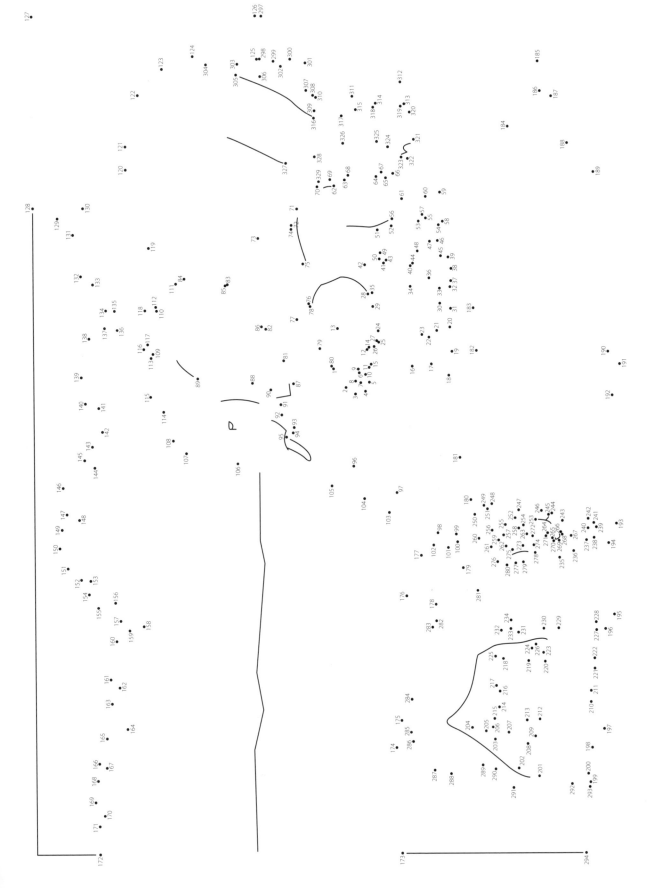

11

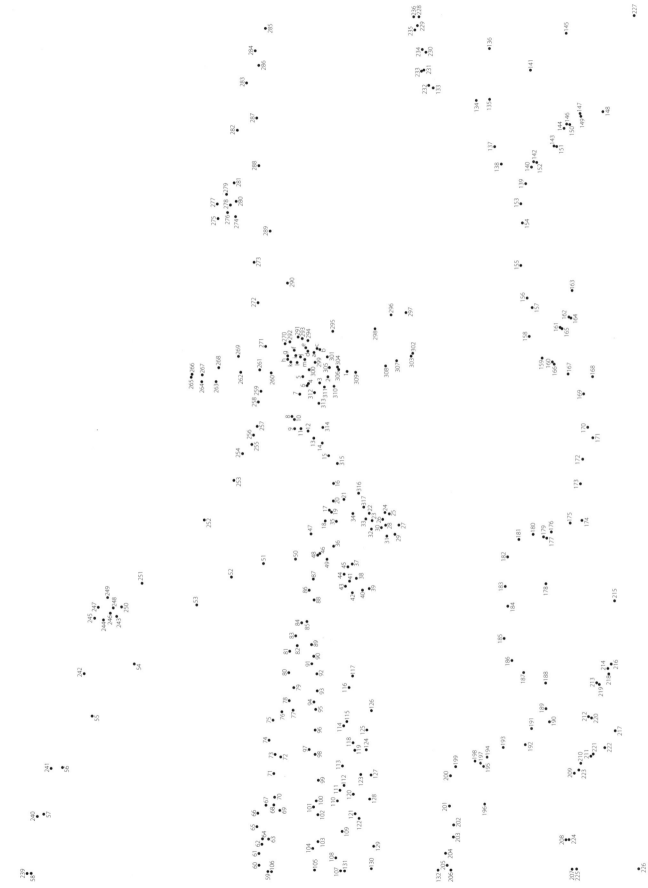

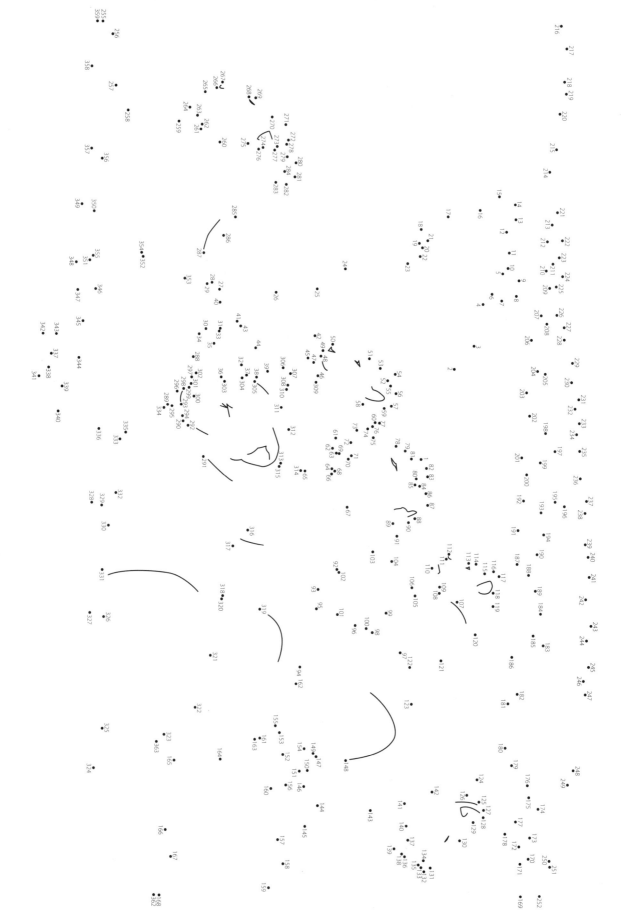

14

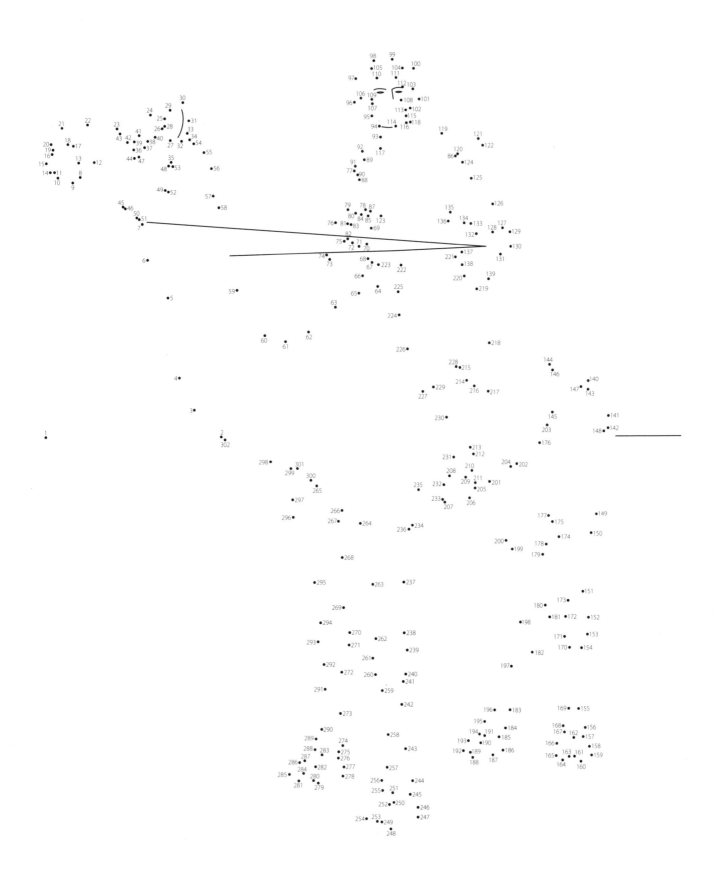

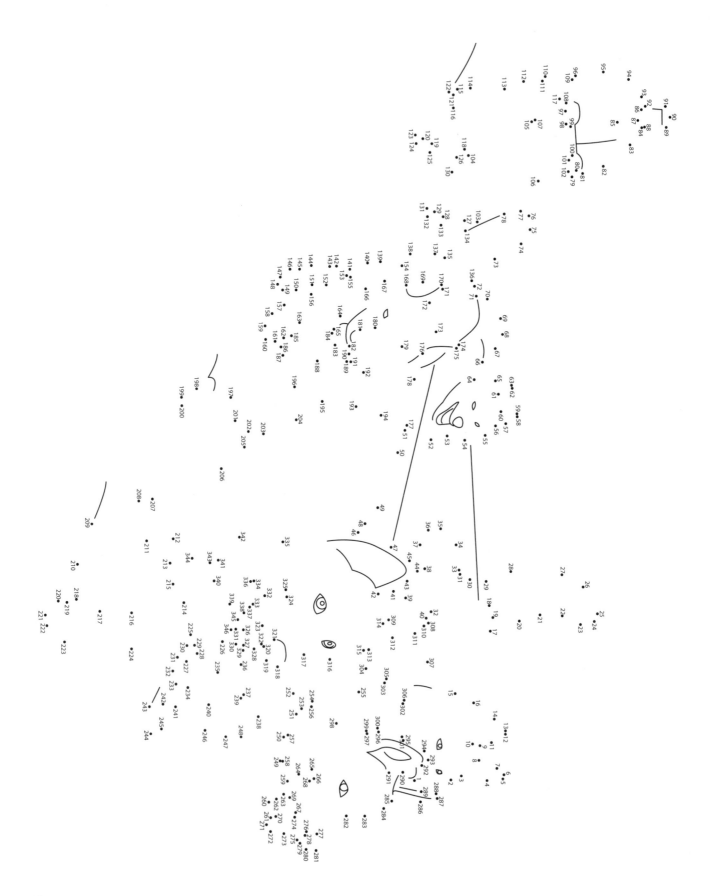

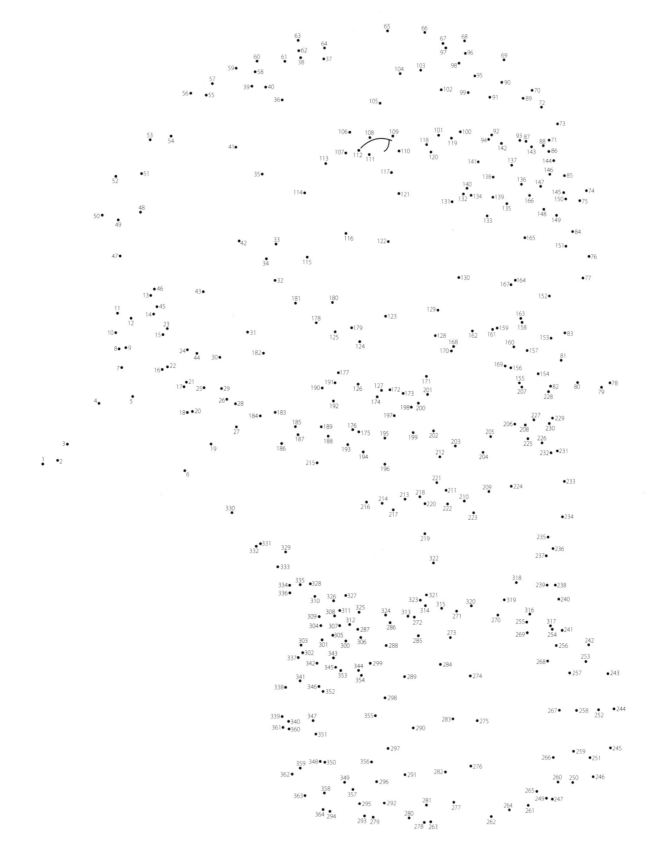

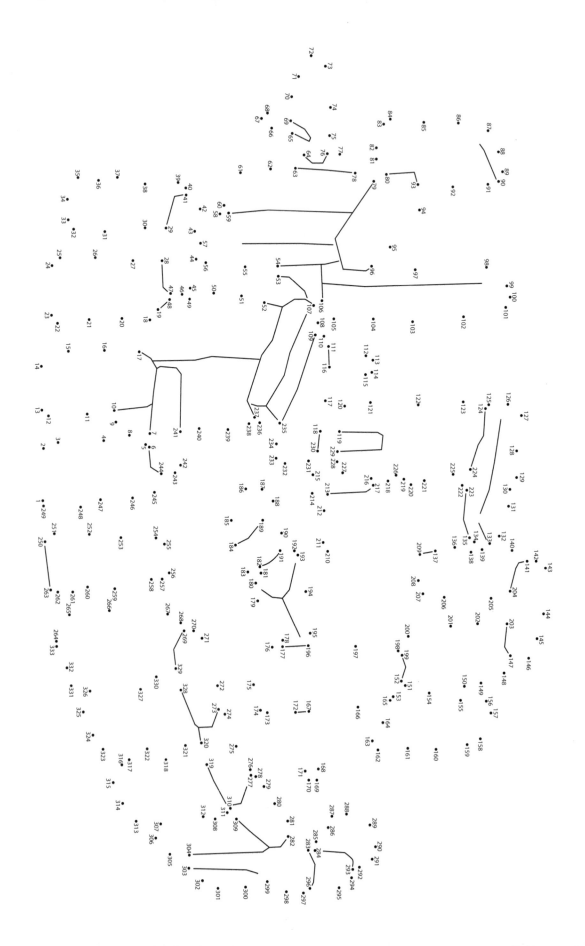

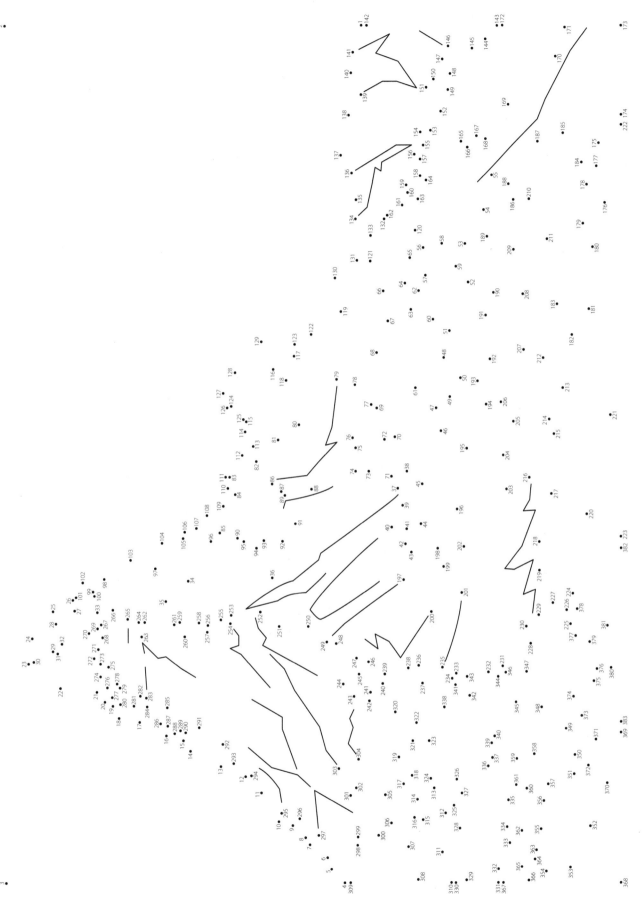

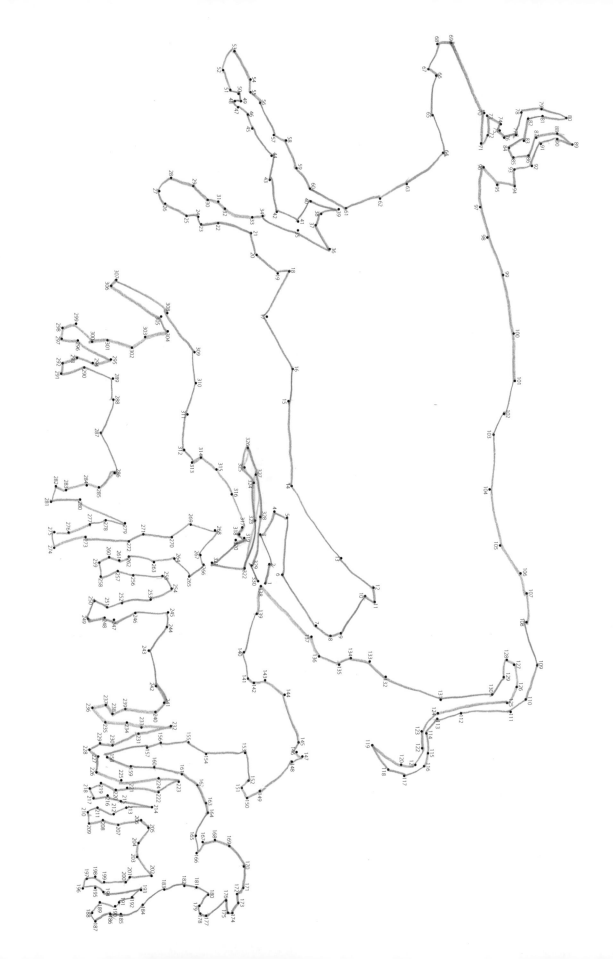

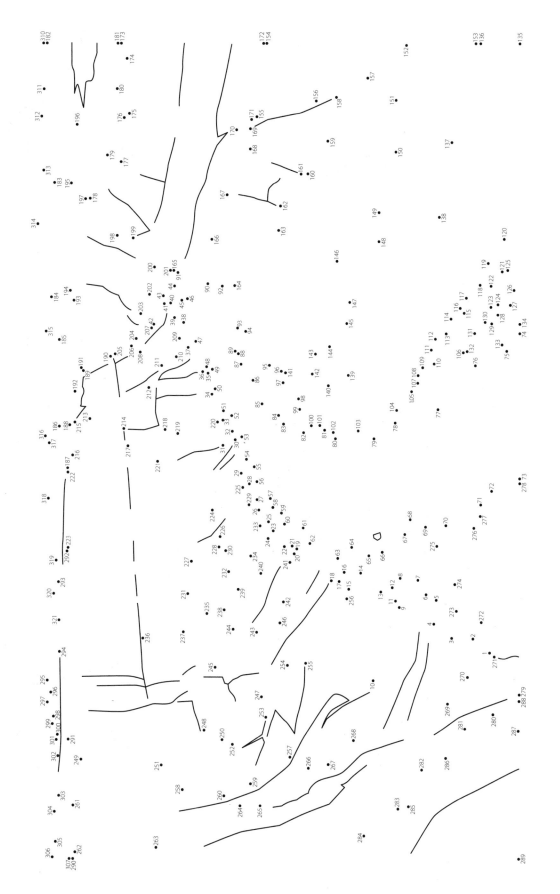

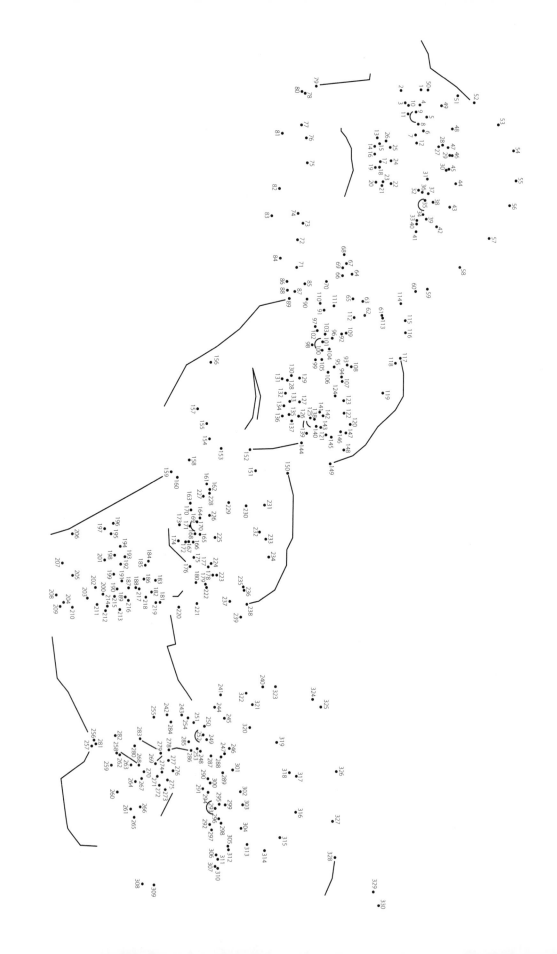

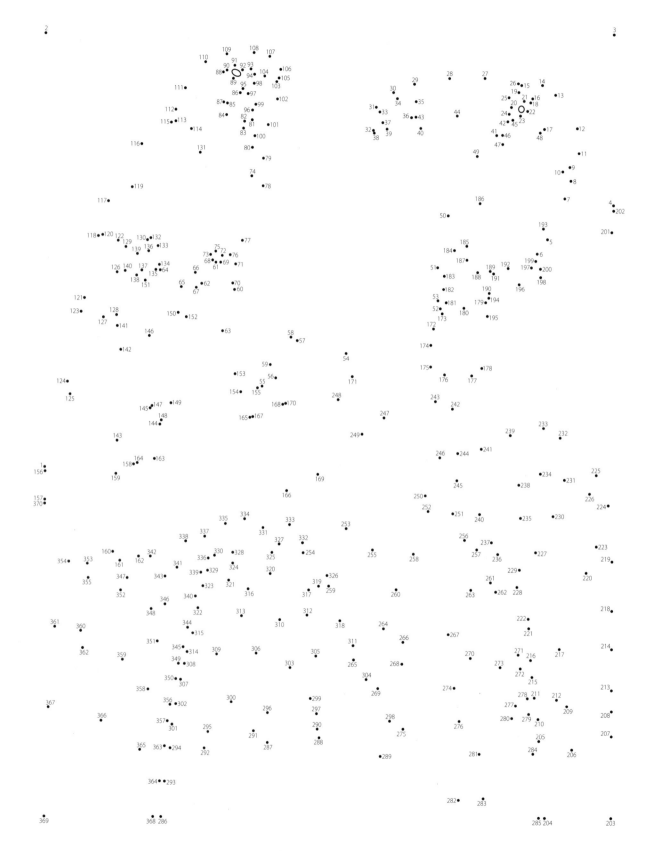

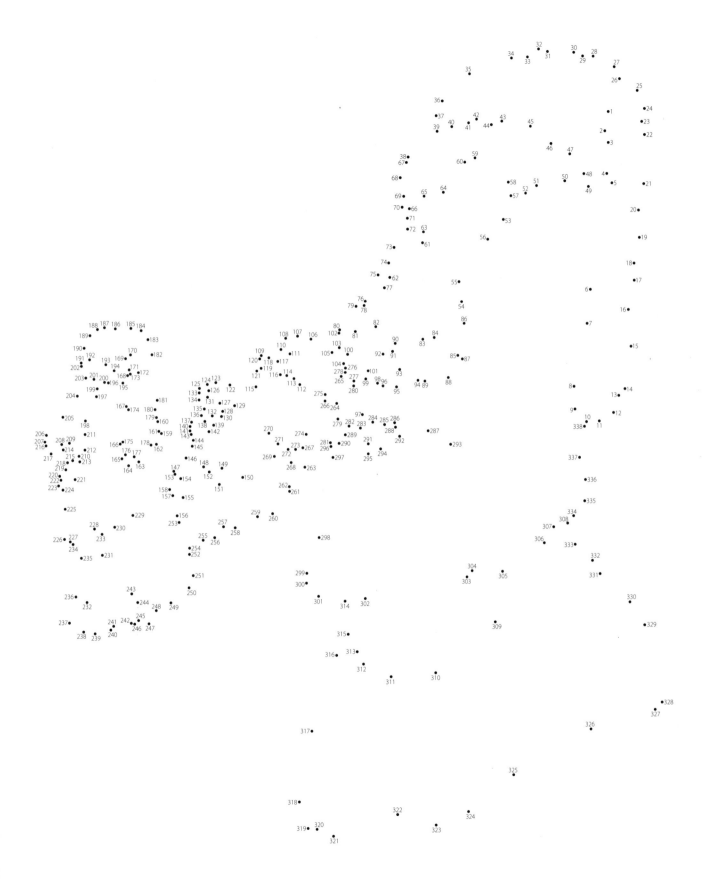

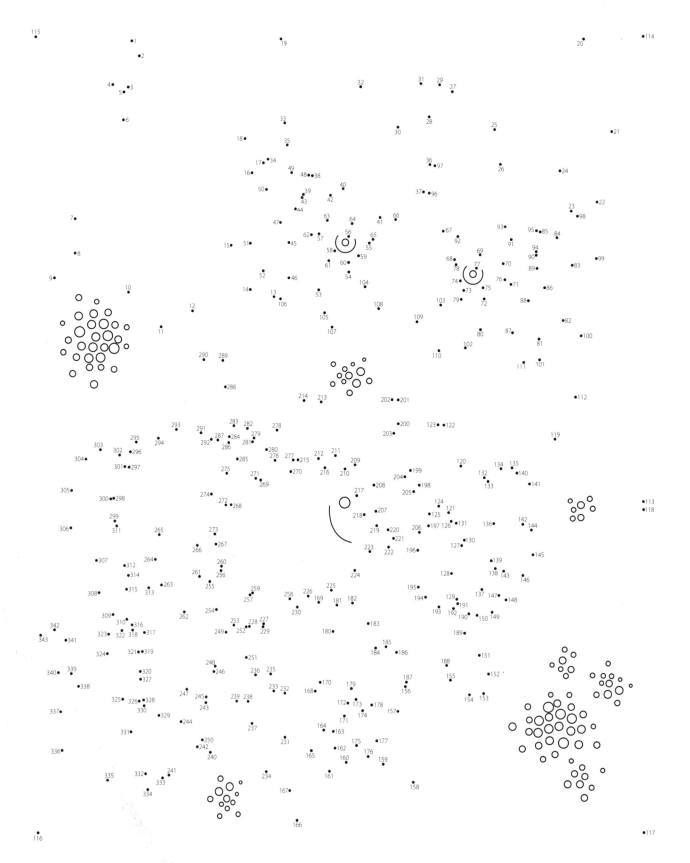

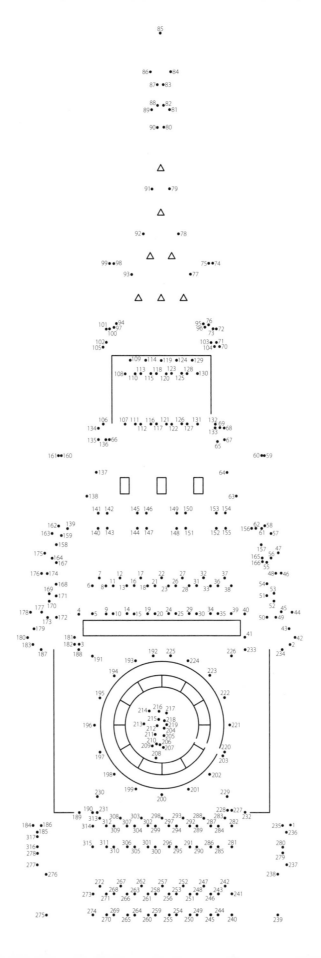

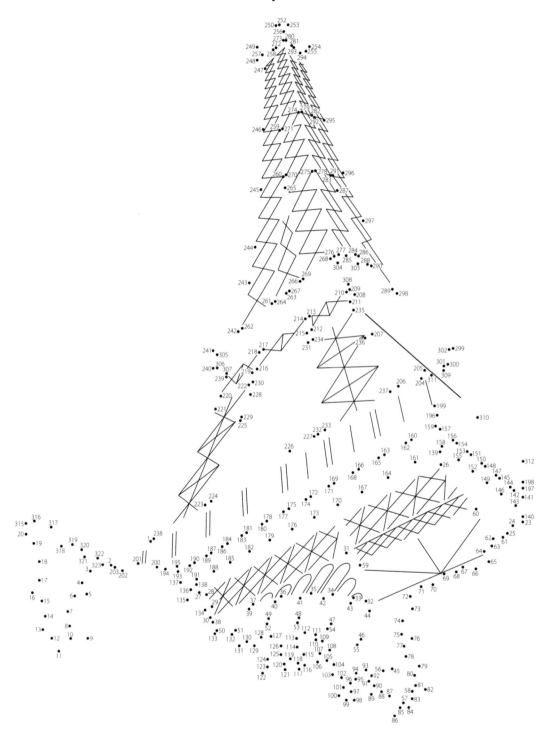

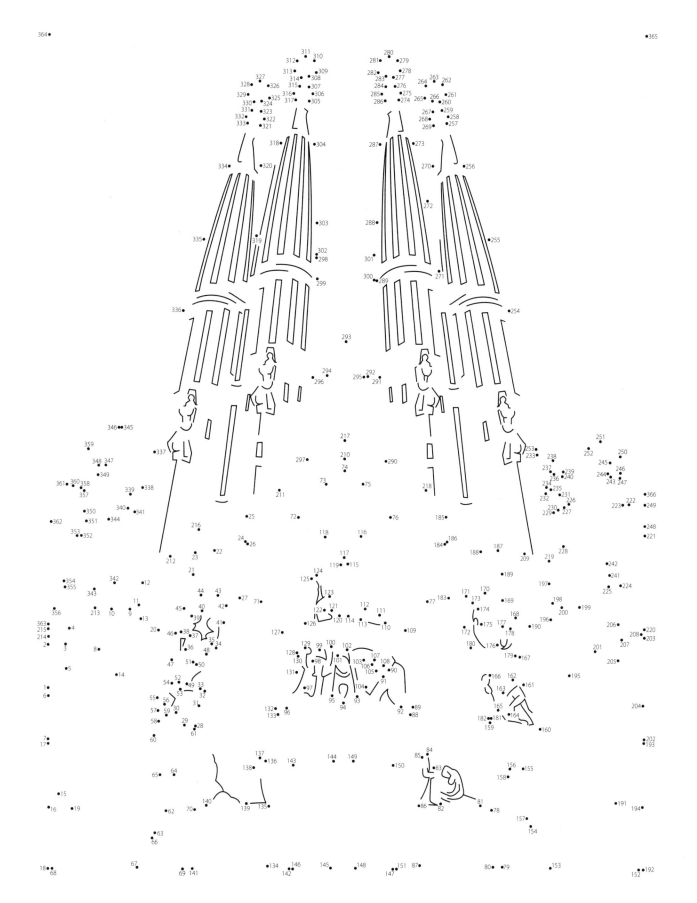

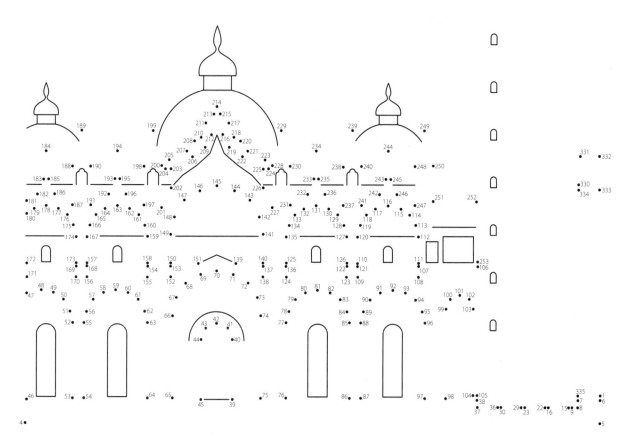
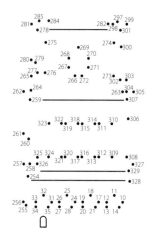

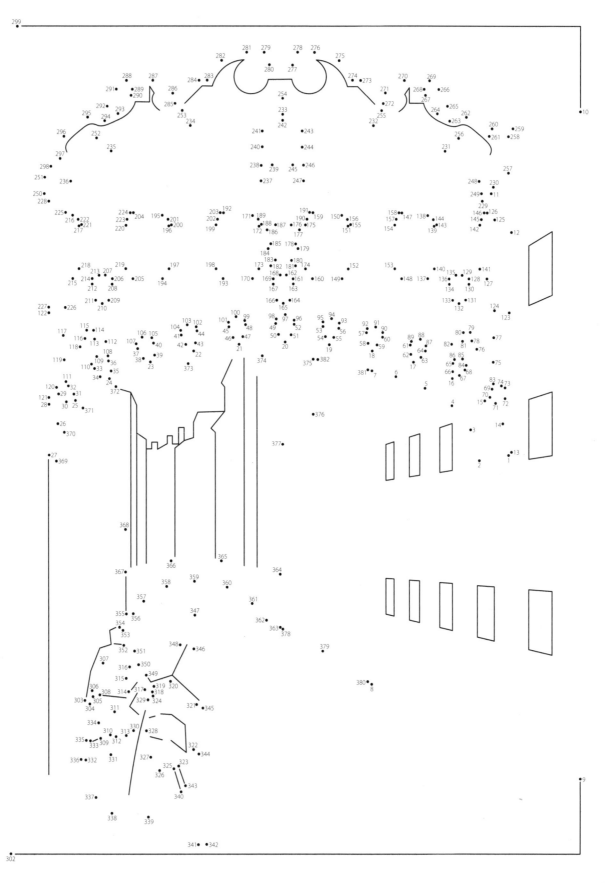

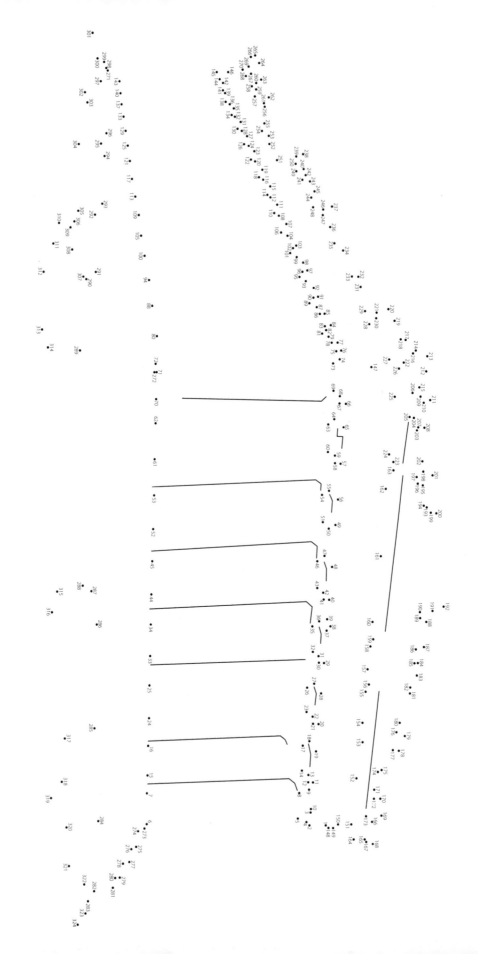

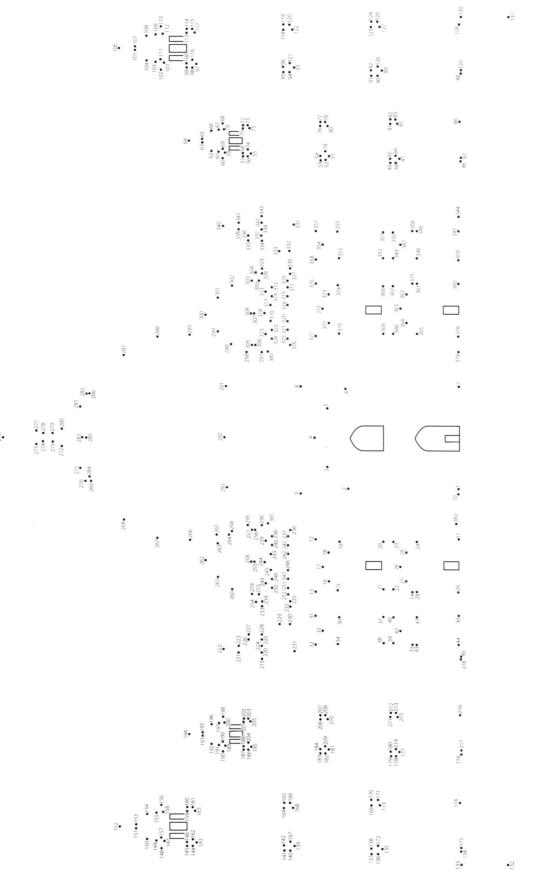

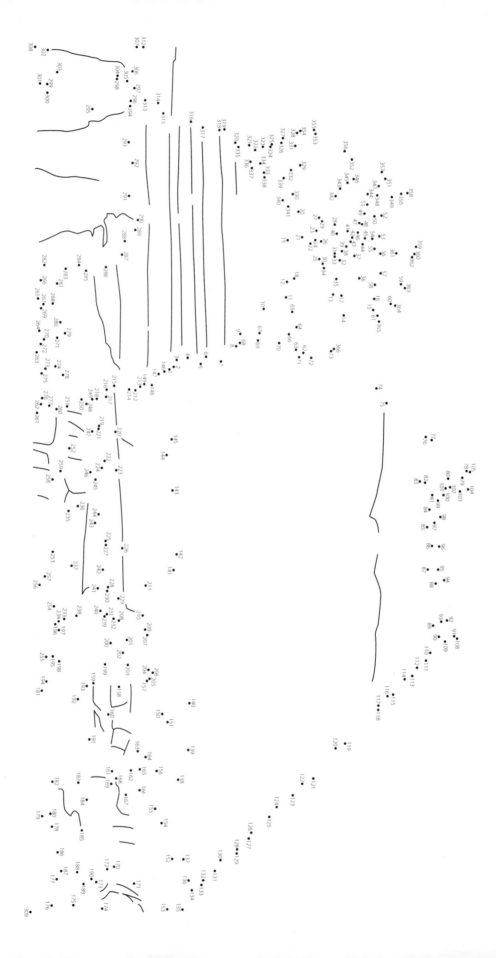

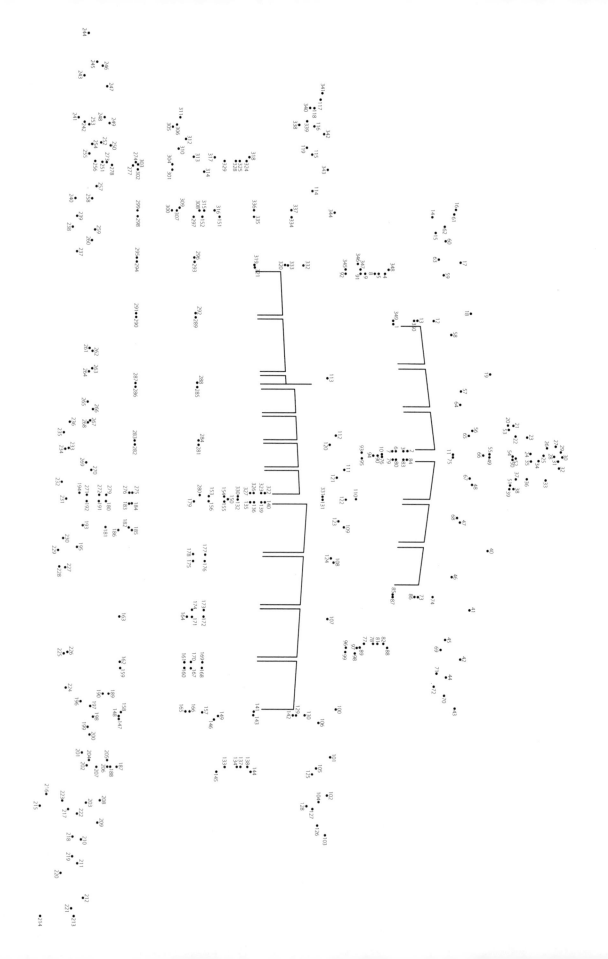

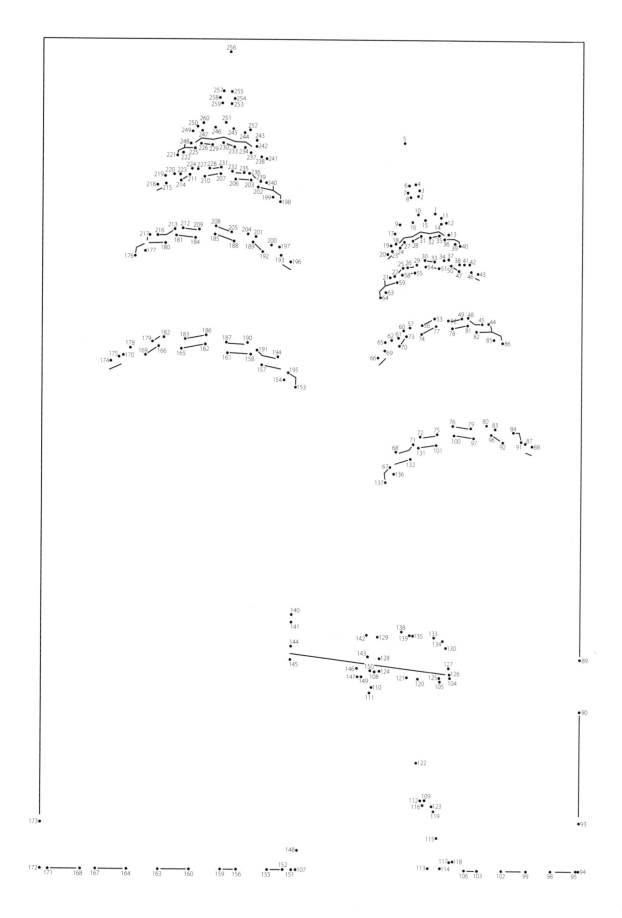

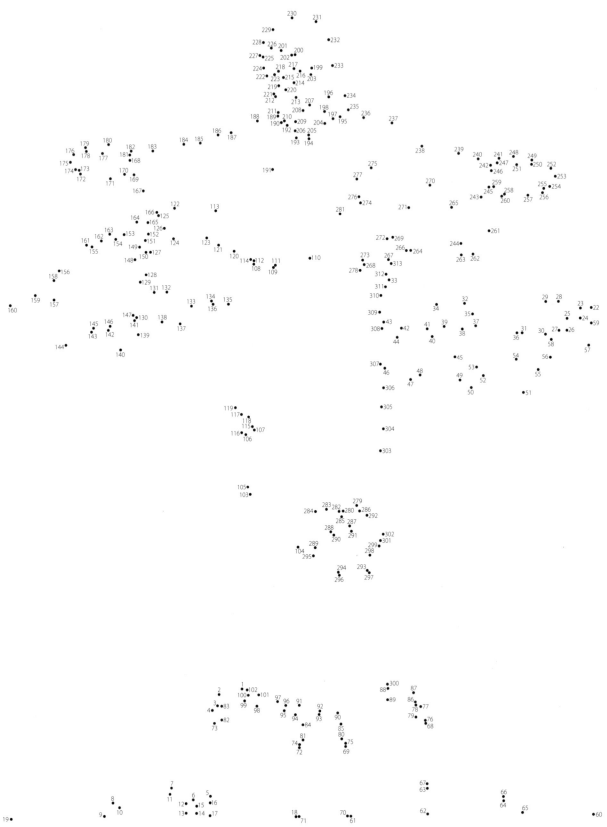

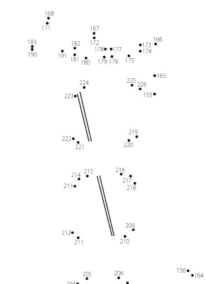

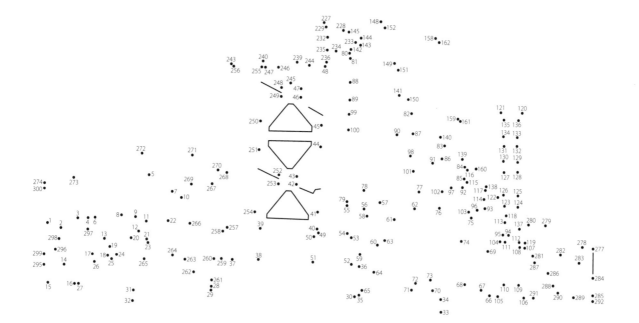

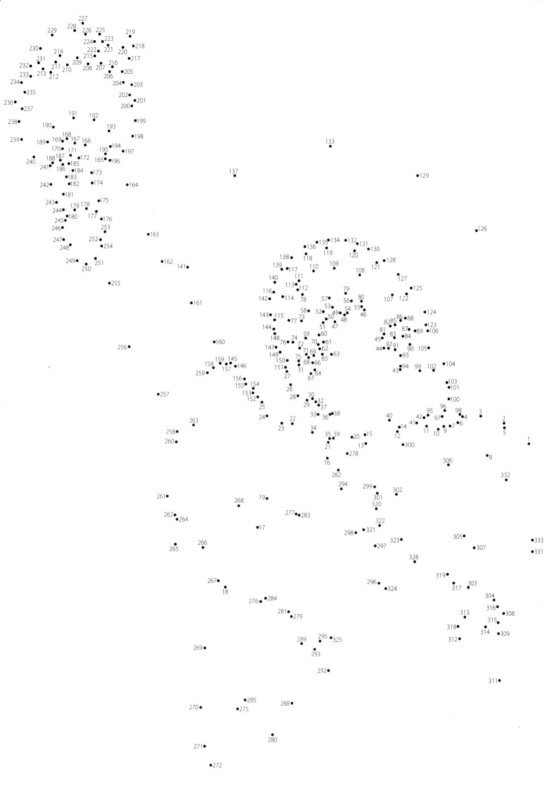

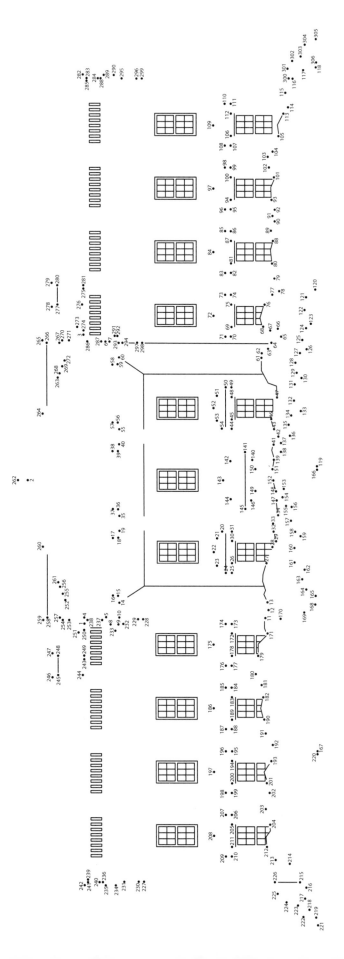

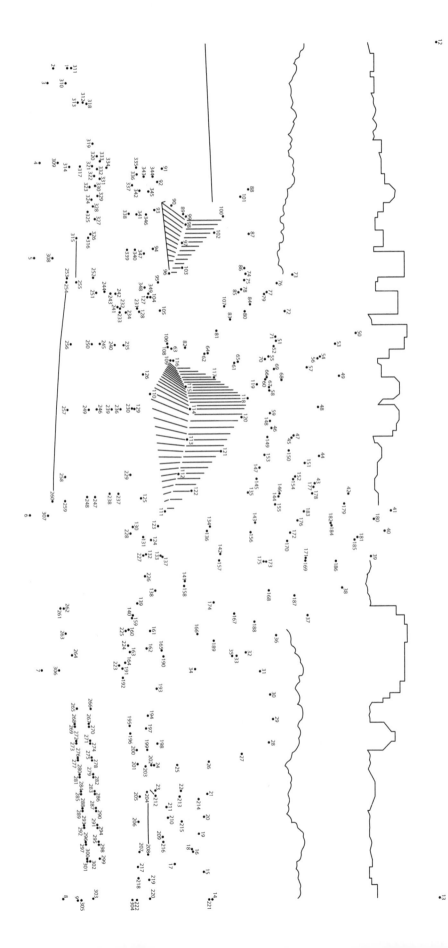

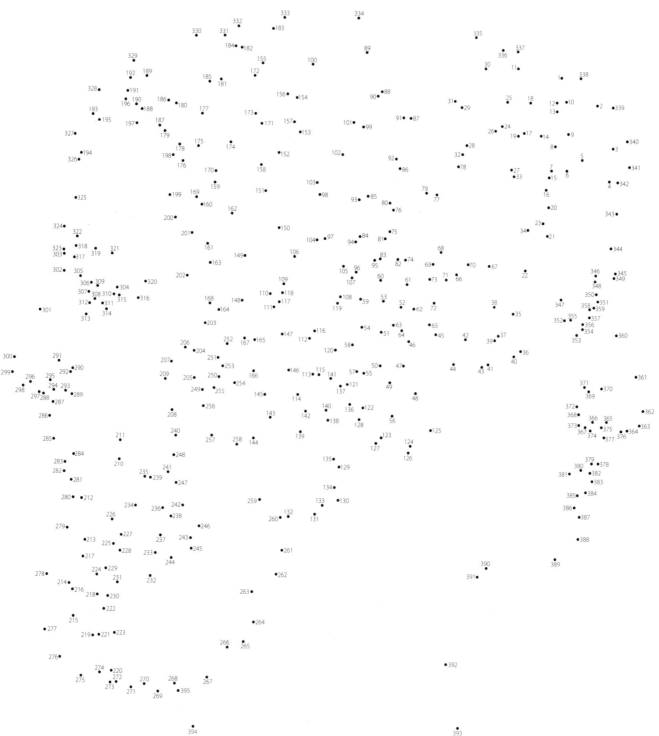

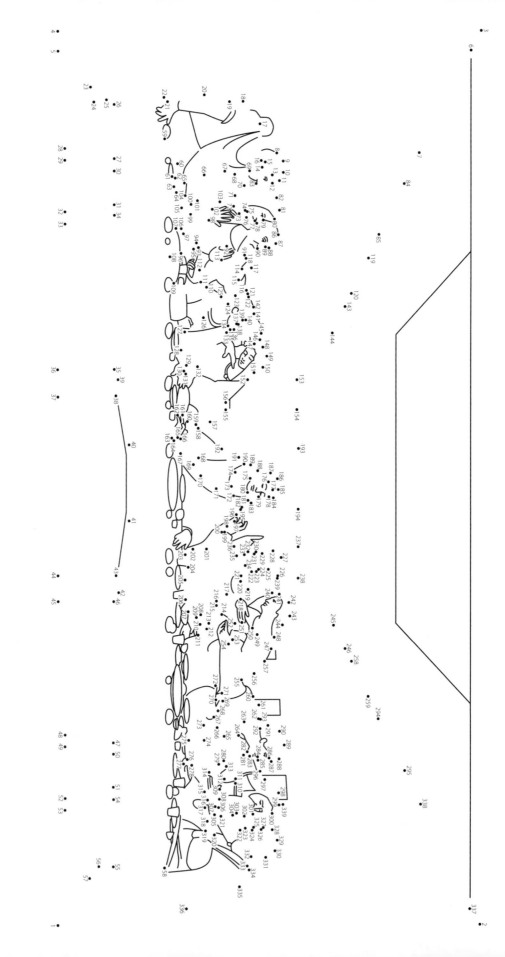

This picture is made from 2 continuous lines:
a) numbers and b) lower case letters

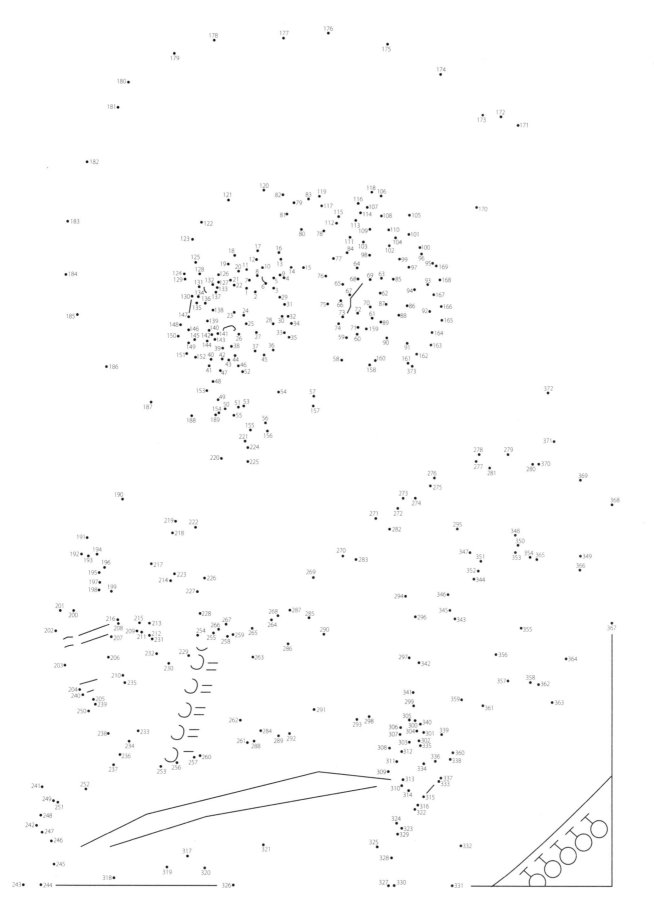

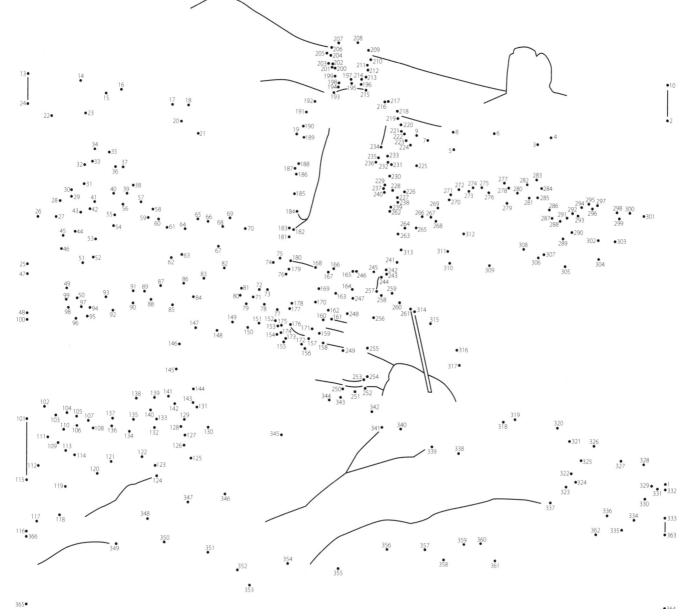

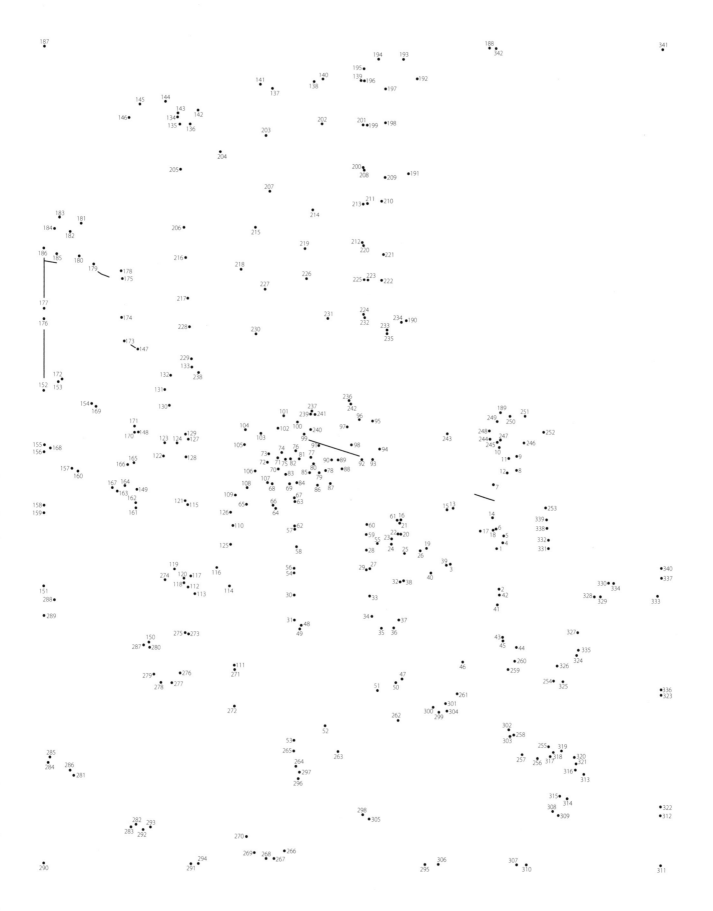

This picture is made from 3 continuous lines:
a) numbers, b) upper case letters and c) lower case letters

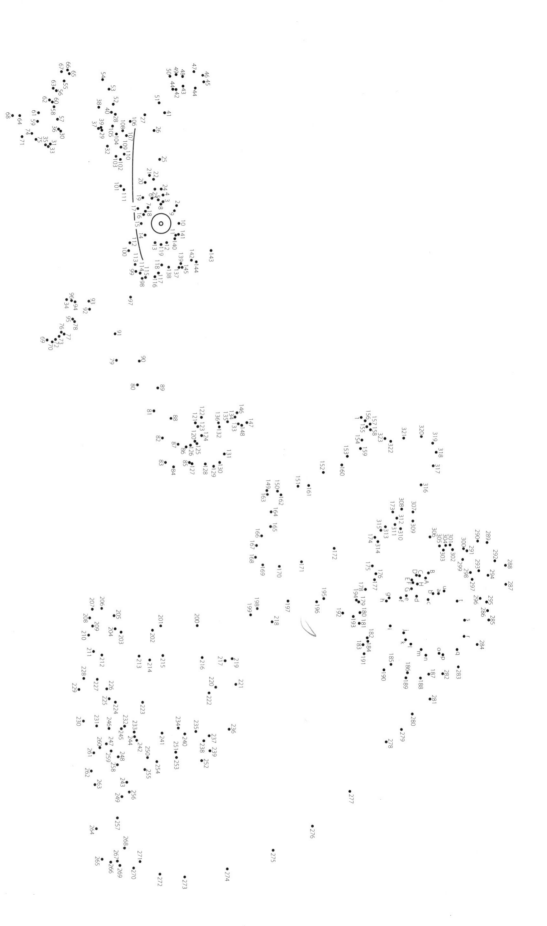

This picture is made from 4 continuous lines:
a) numbers, b) upper case letters, c) lower case letters and d) roman numerals

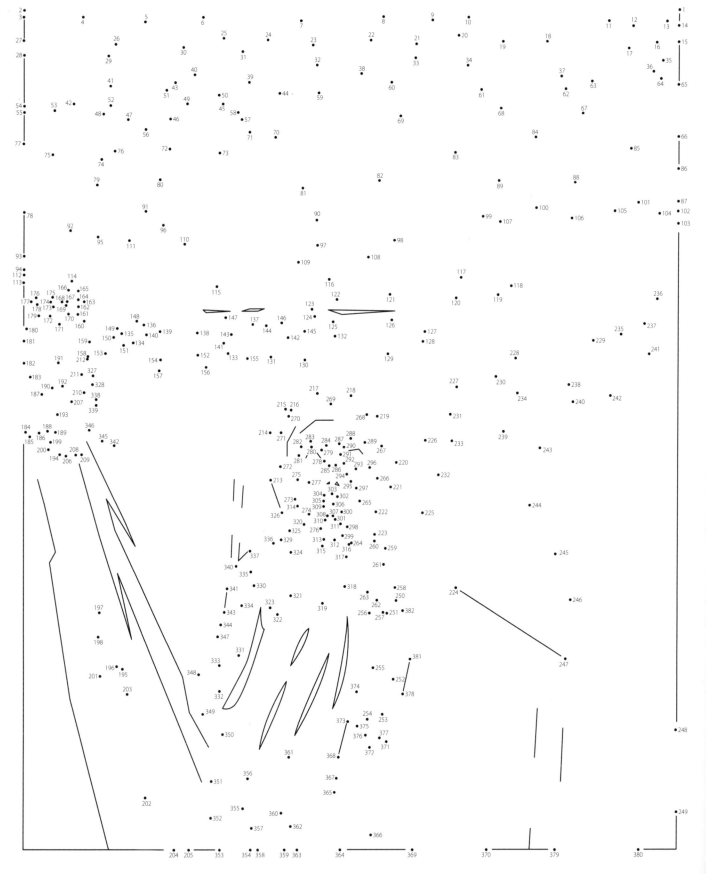

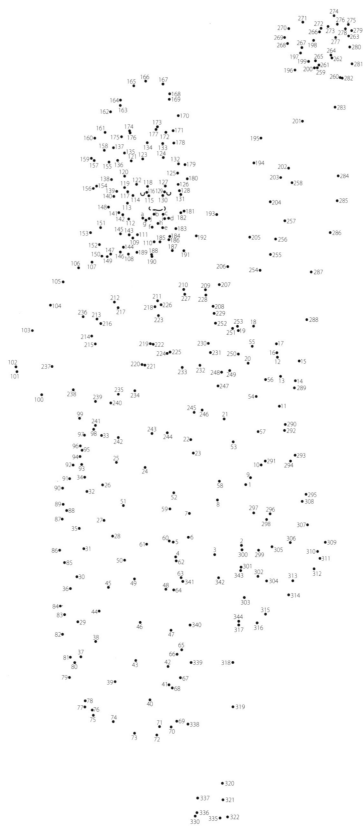

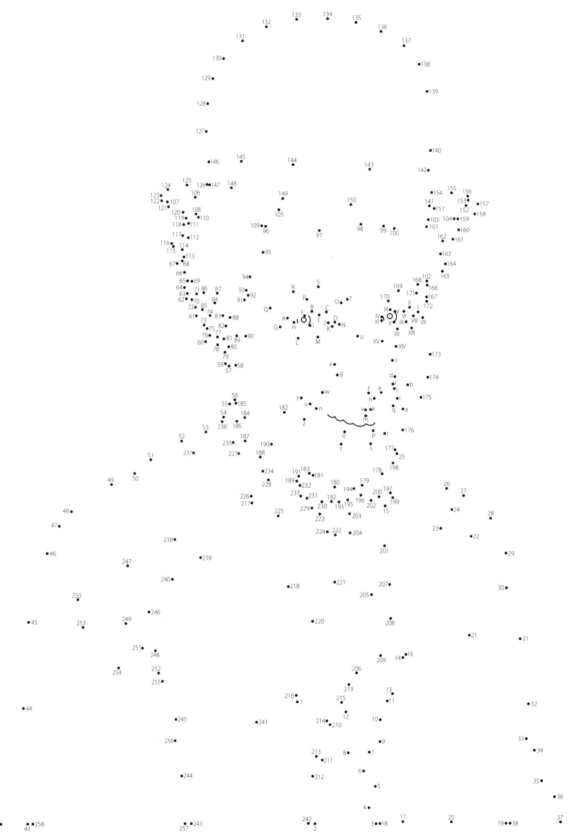

This picture is made from 4 continuous lines:
a) numbers, b) upper case letters, c) lower case letters and d) roman numerals

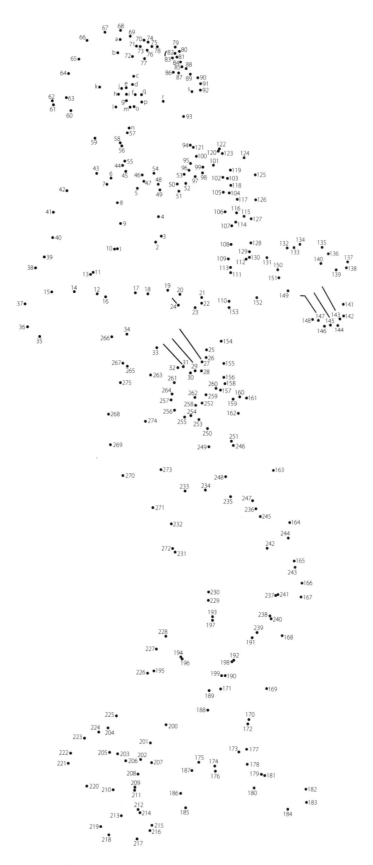

This picture is made from 2 continuous lines:
a) numbers and b) lower case letters

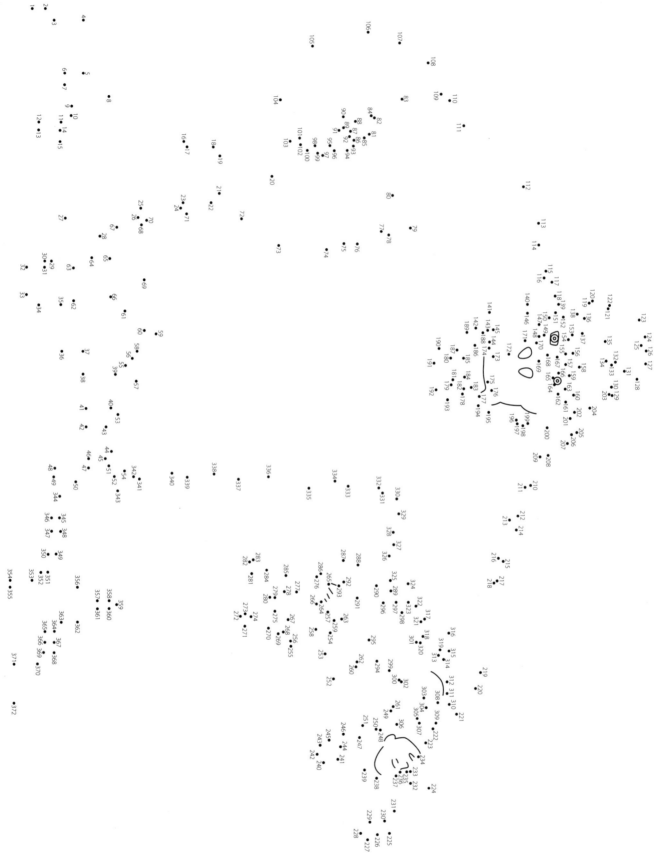

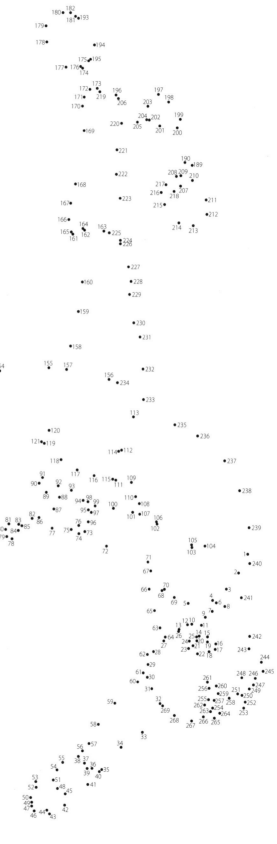
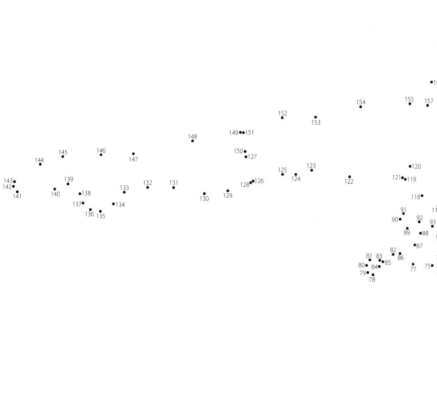

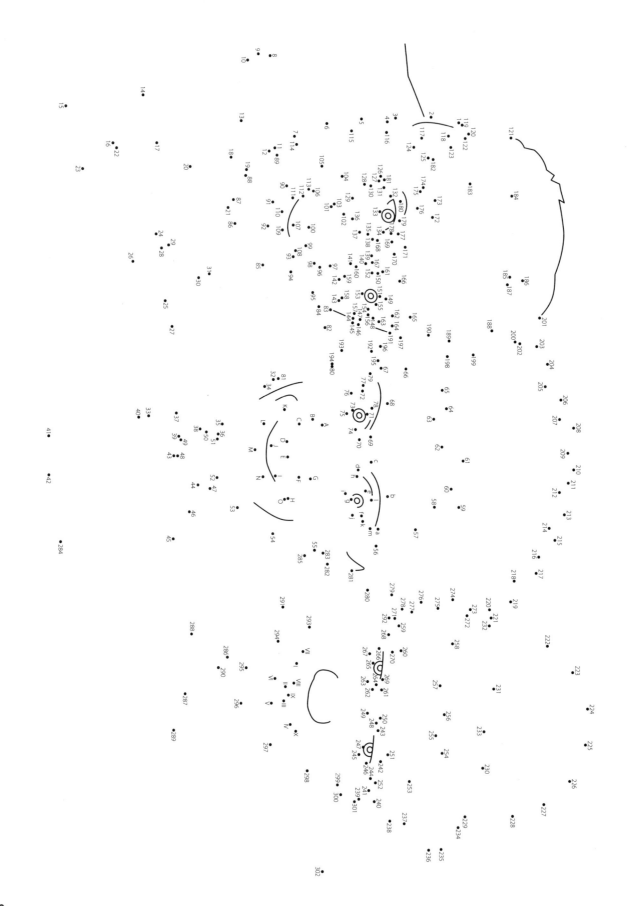

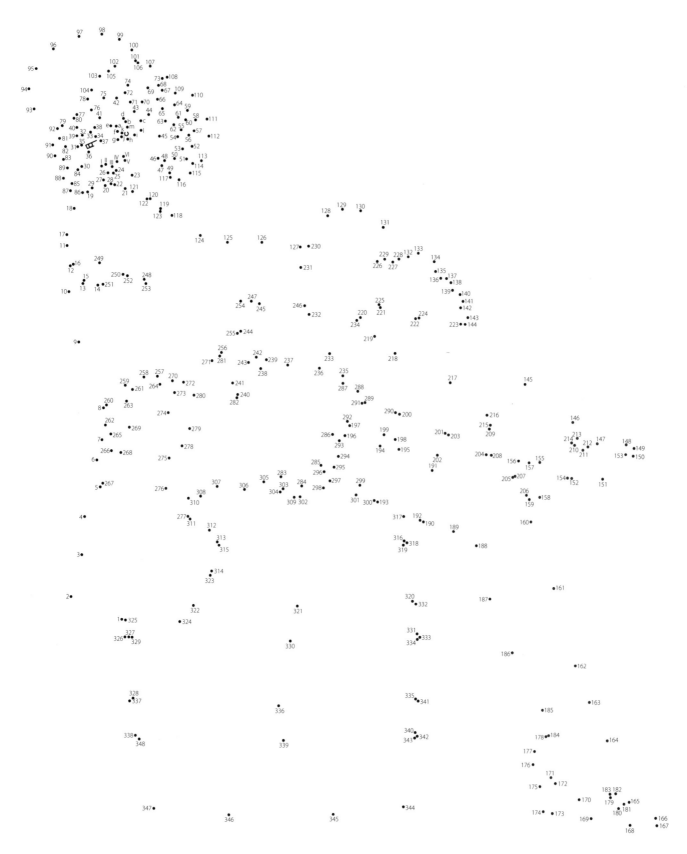

This picture is made from 3 continuous lines:
a) numbers, b) lower case letters and c) roman numerals

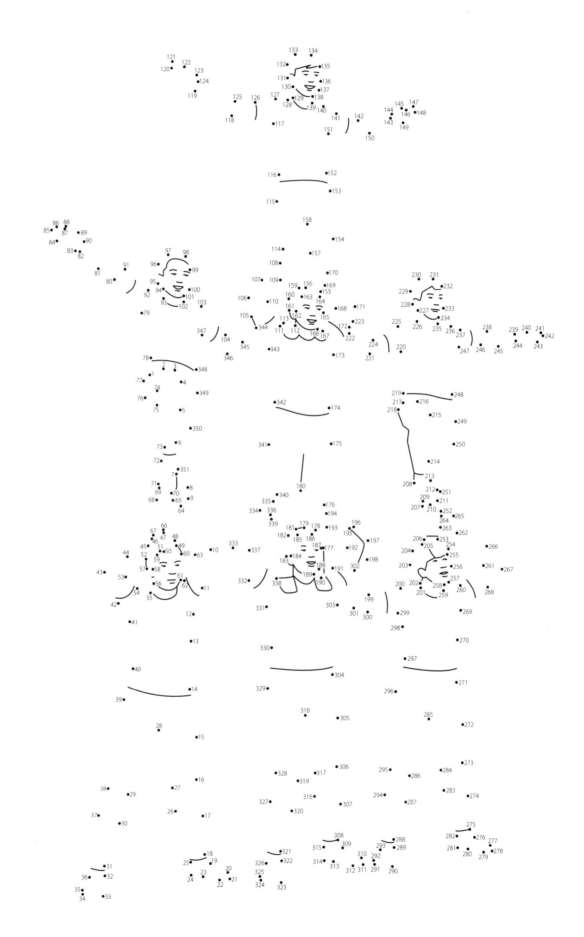

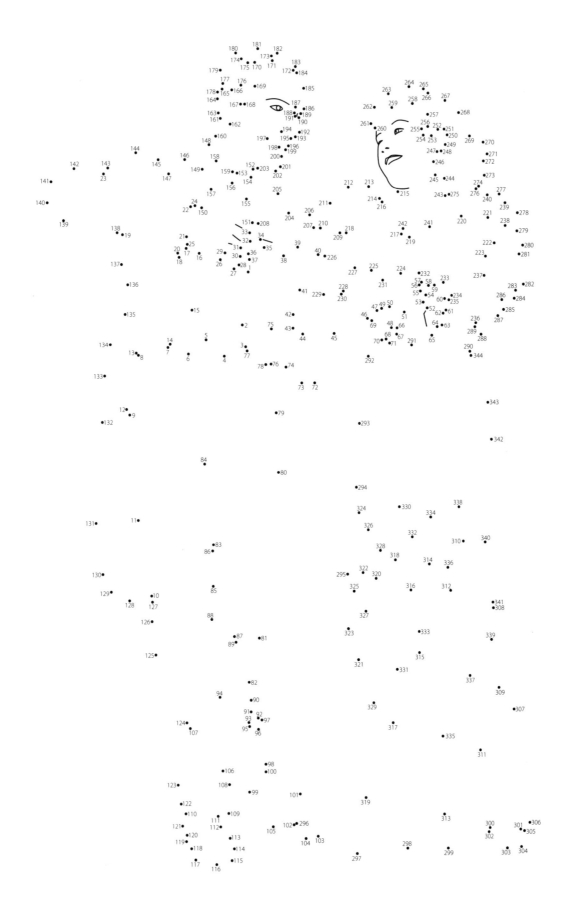

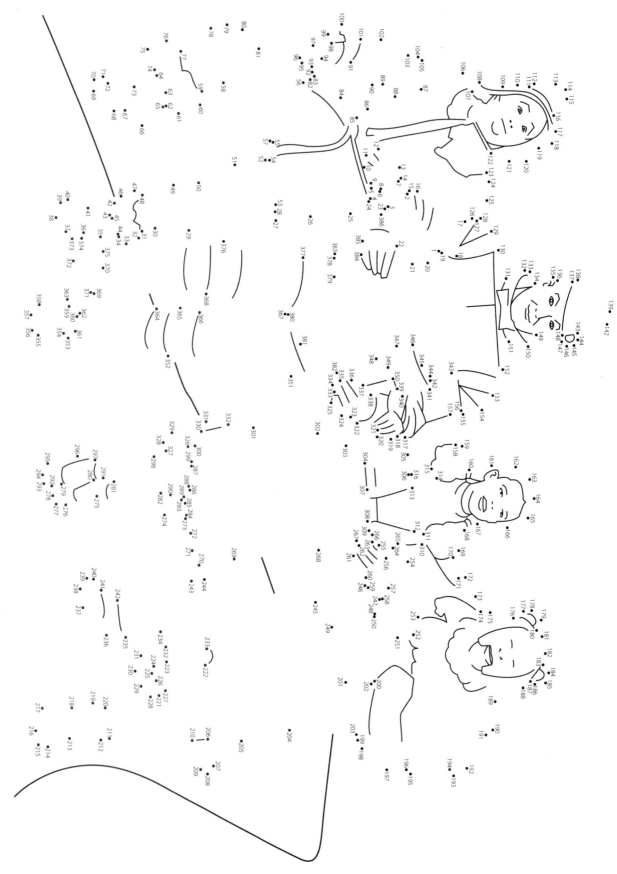

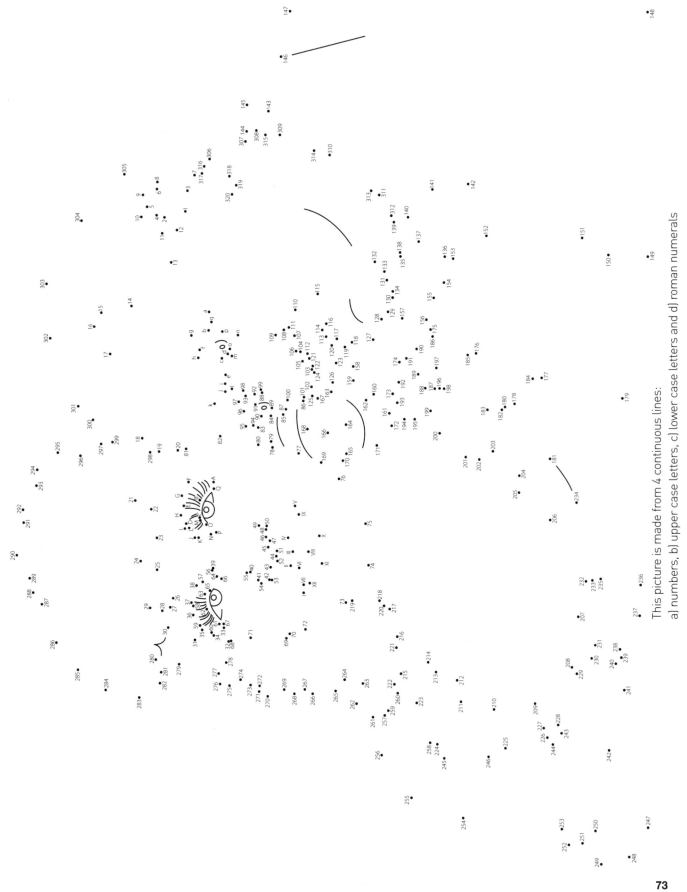

This picture is made from 4 continuous lines:
a) numbers, b) upper case letters, c) lower case letters and d) roman numerals

73

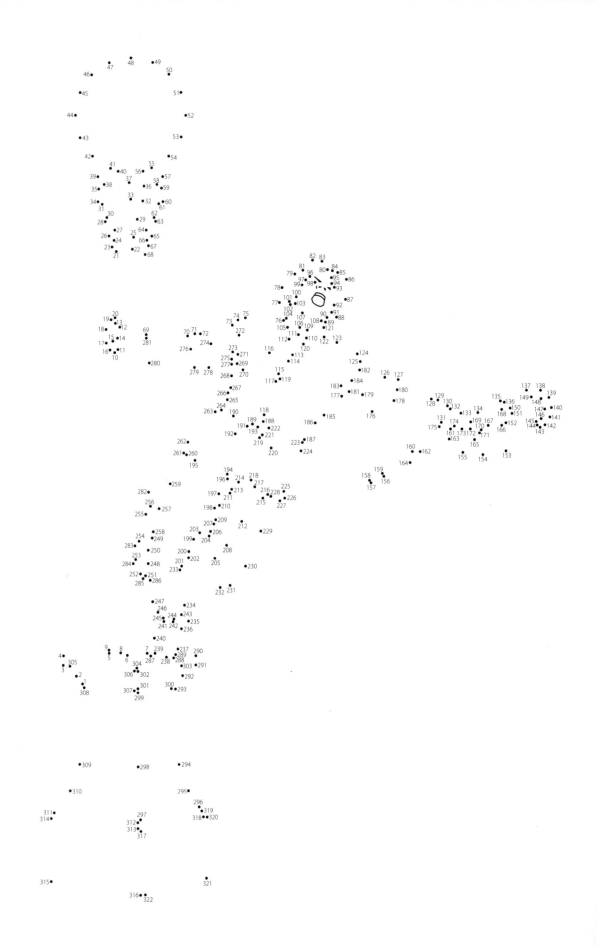

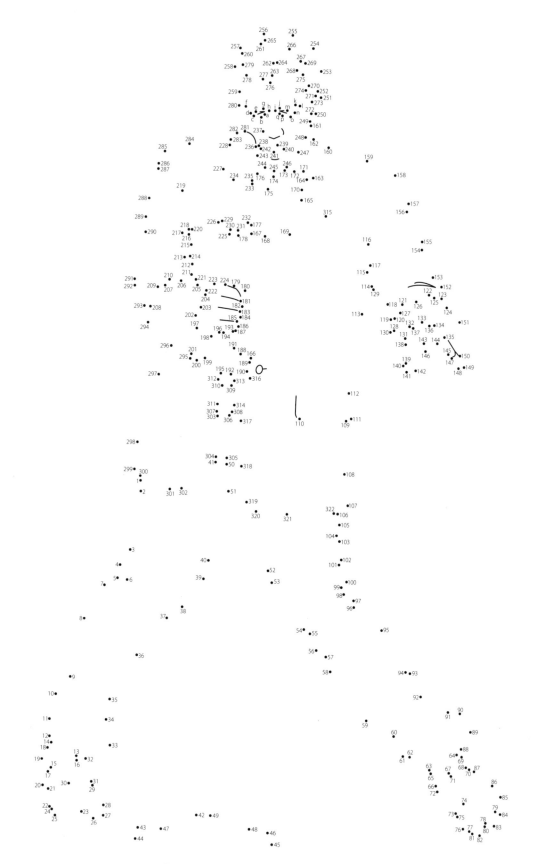

This picture is made from 2 continuous lines:
a) numbers and b) lower case letters

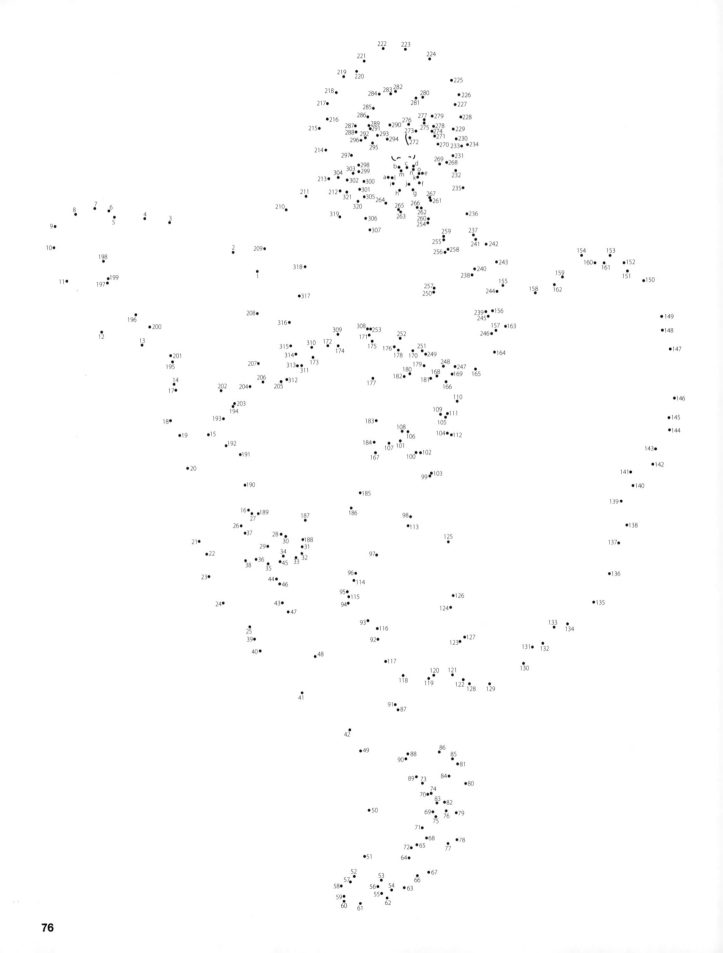

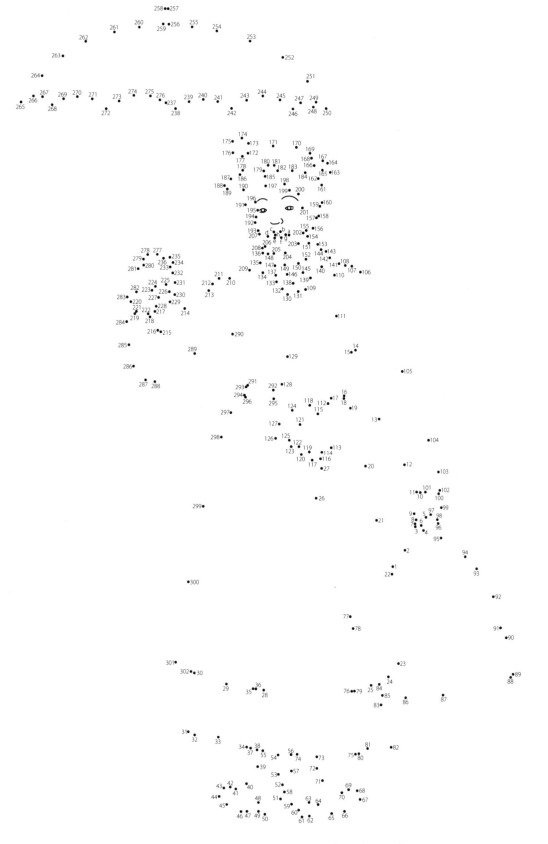

This picture is made from 2 continuous lines:
a) numbers and b) lower case letters

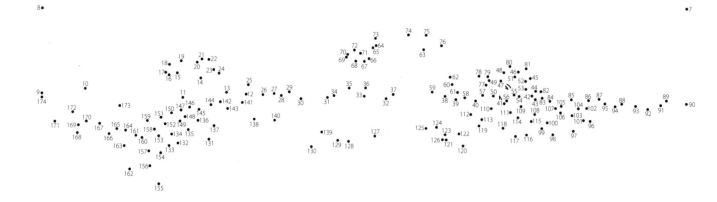
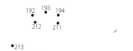

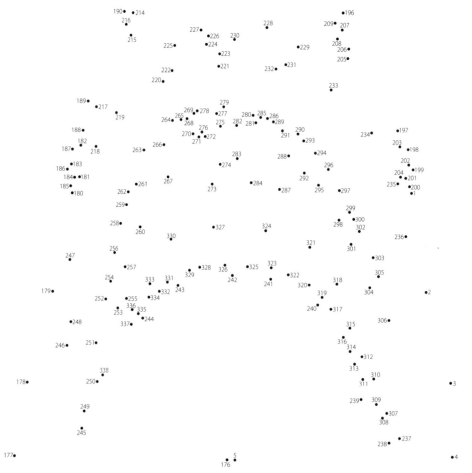

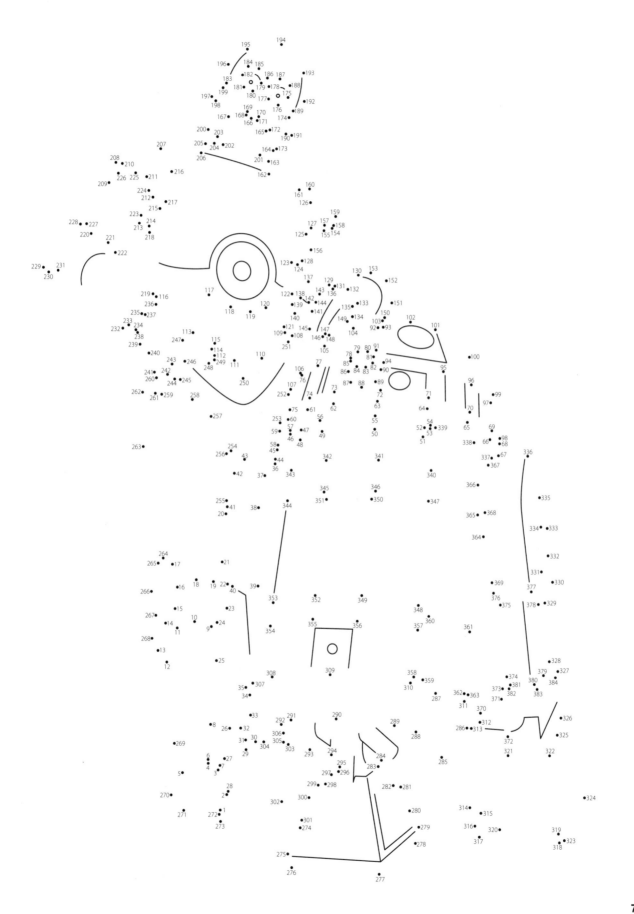

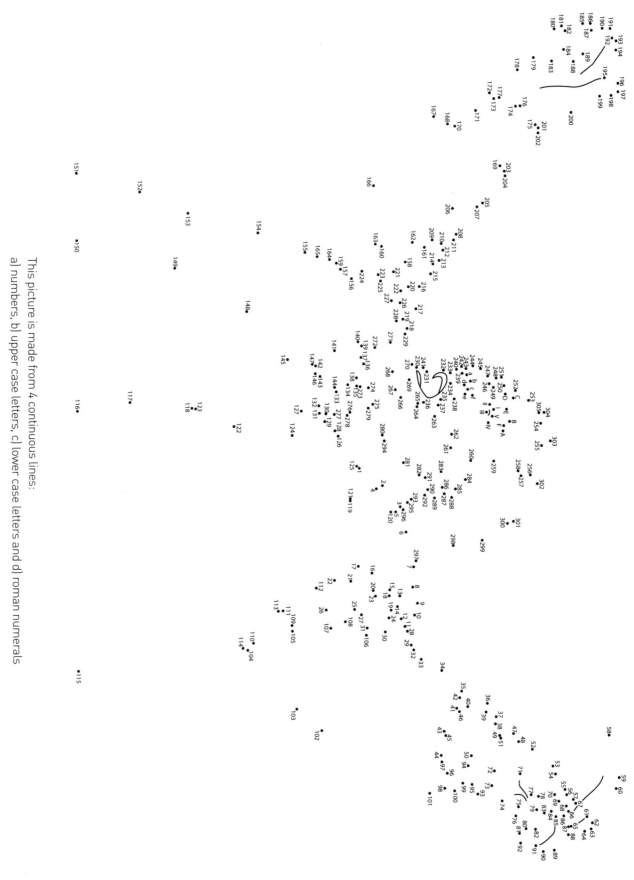

This picture is made from 4 continuous lines:
a) numbers, b) upper case letters, c) lower case letters and d) roman numerals

80

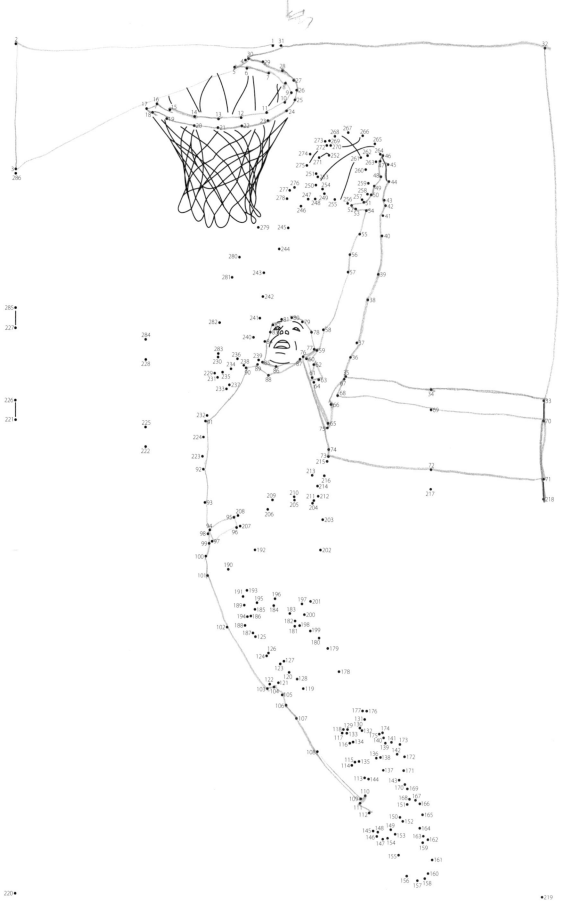

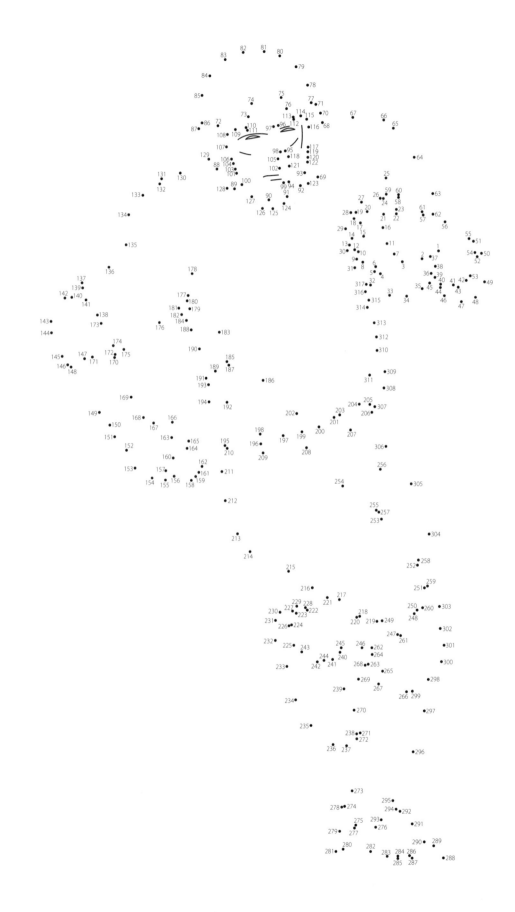

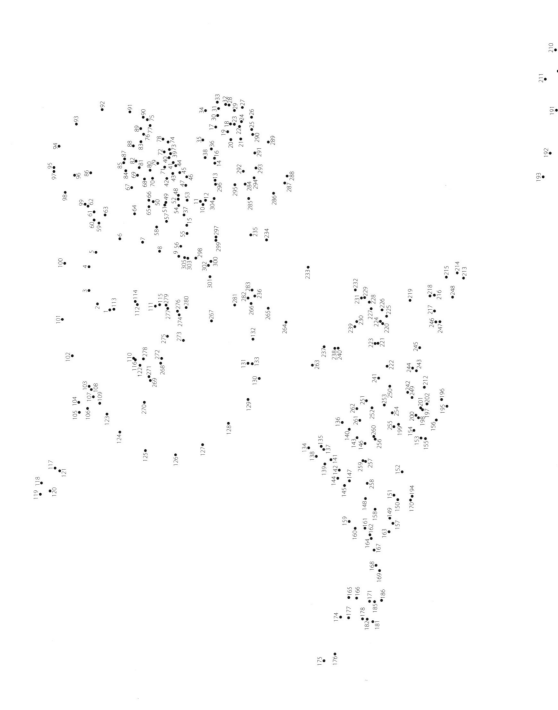

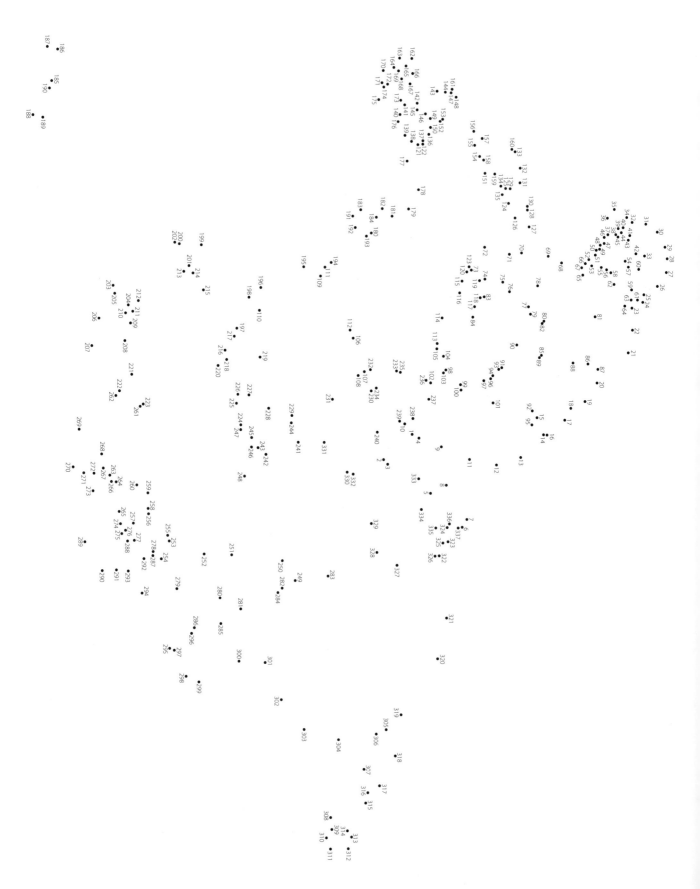

84

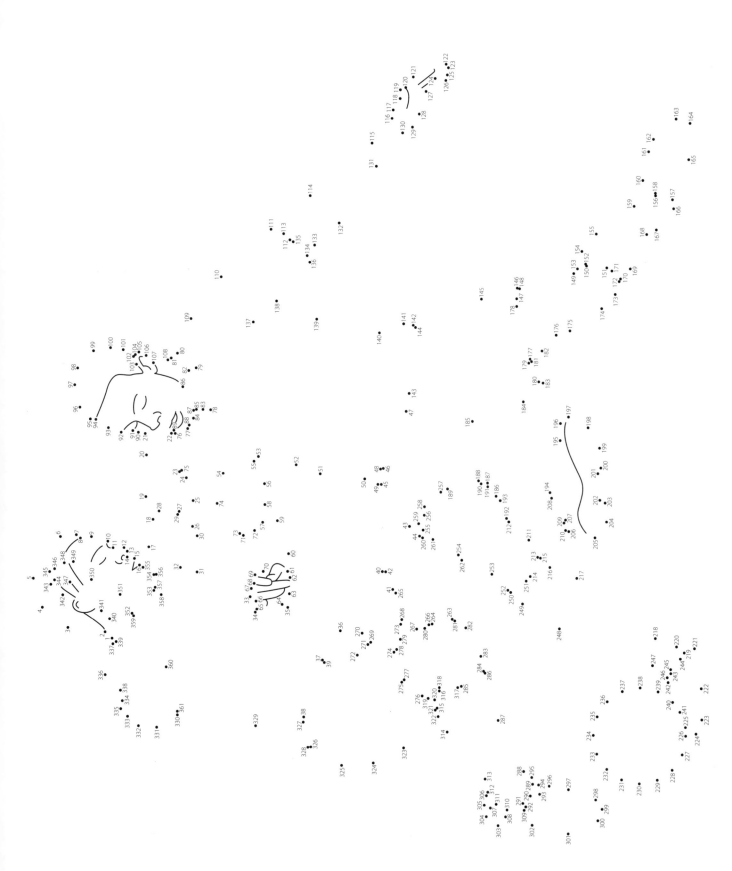

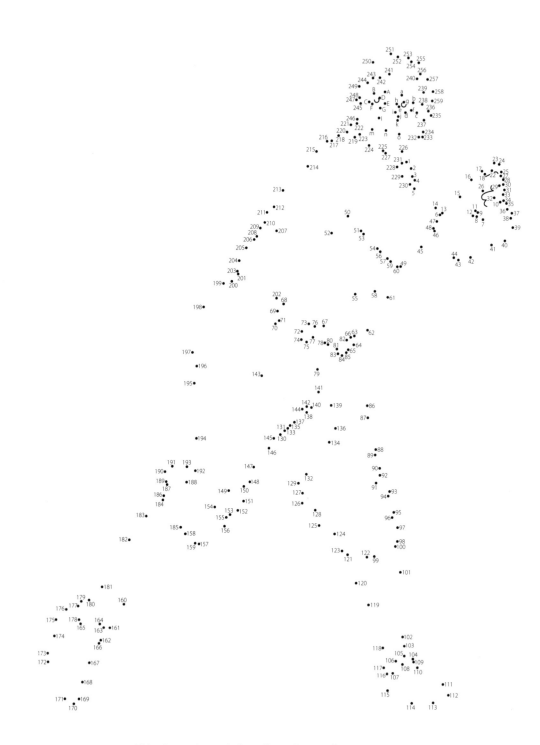

This picture is made from 3 continuous lines:
a) numbers, b) upper case letters and c) lower case letters

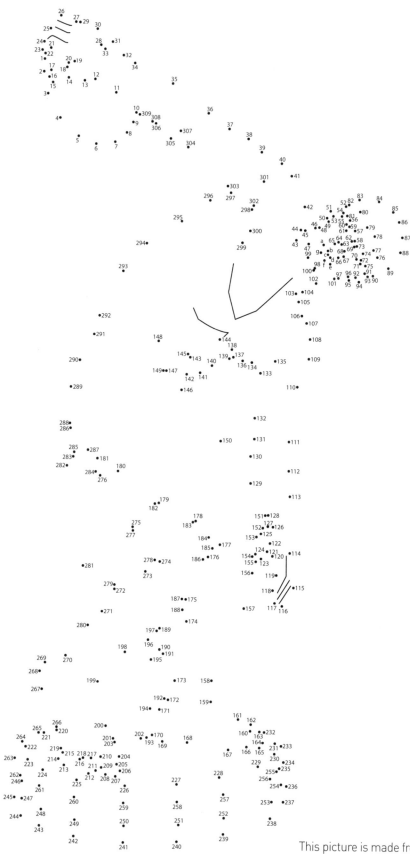

This picture is made from 2 continuous lines:
a) numbers and b) lower case letters

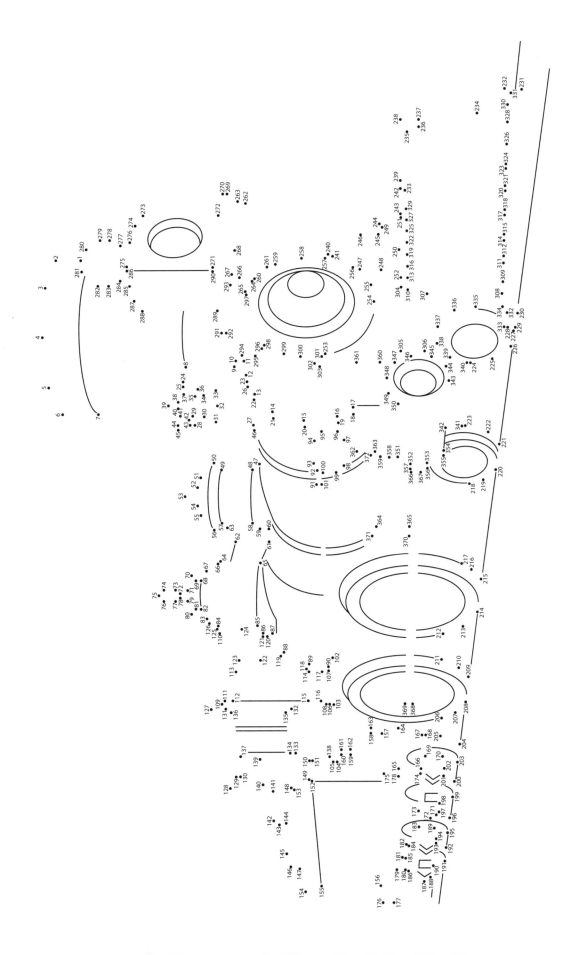

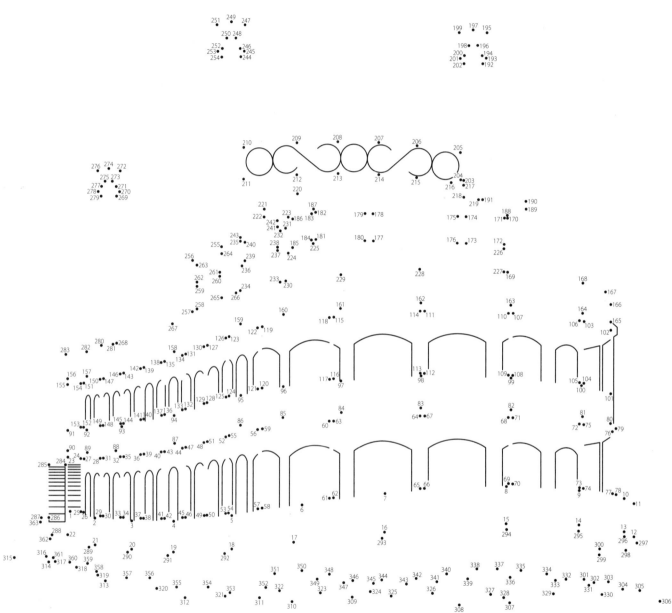

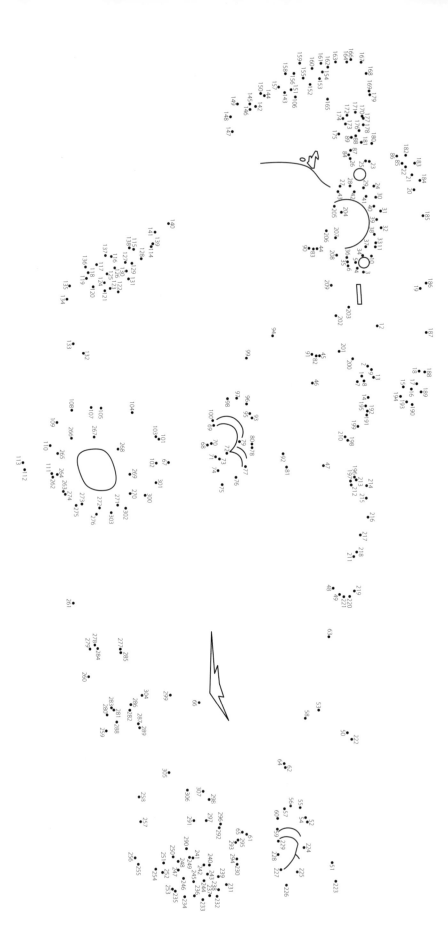

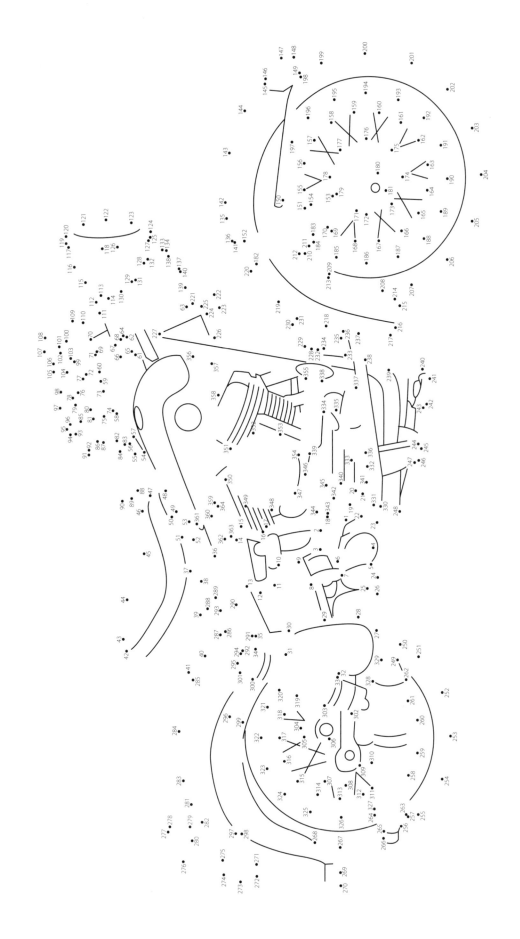

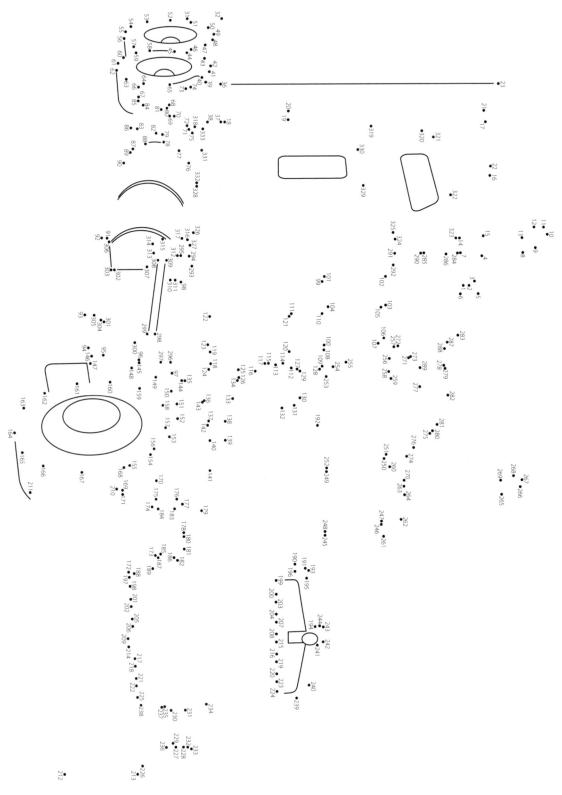

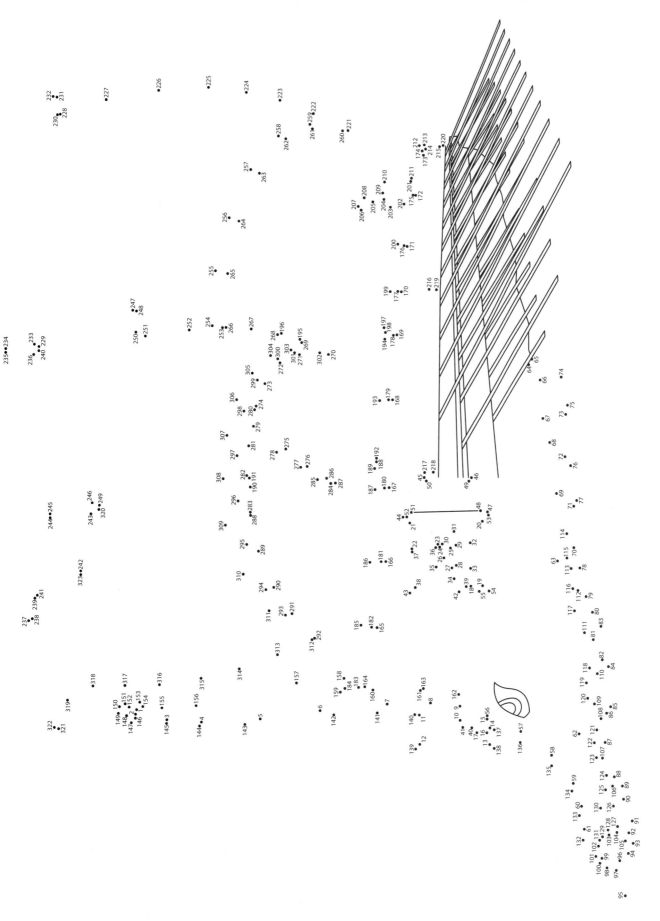

97

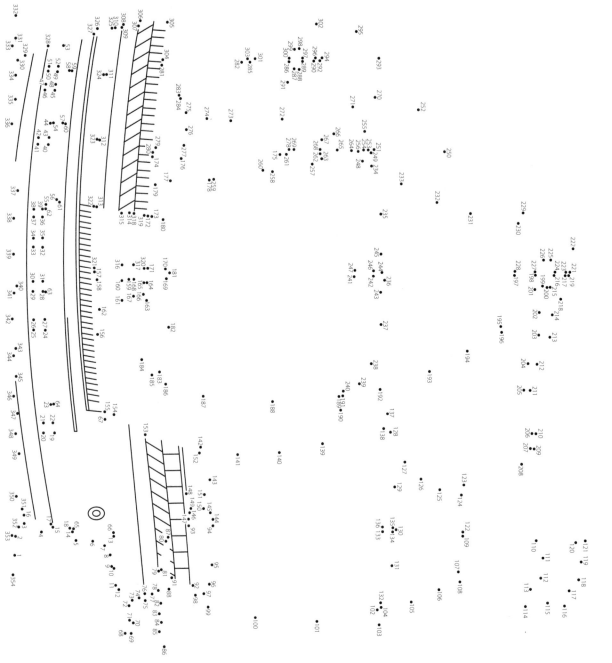

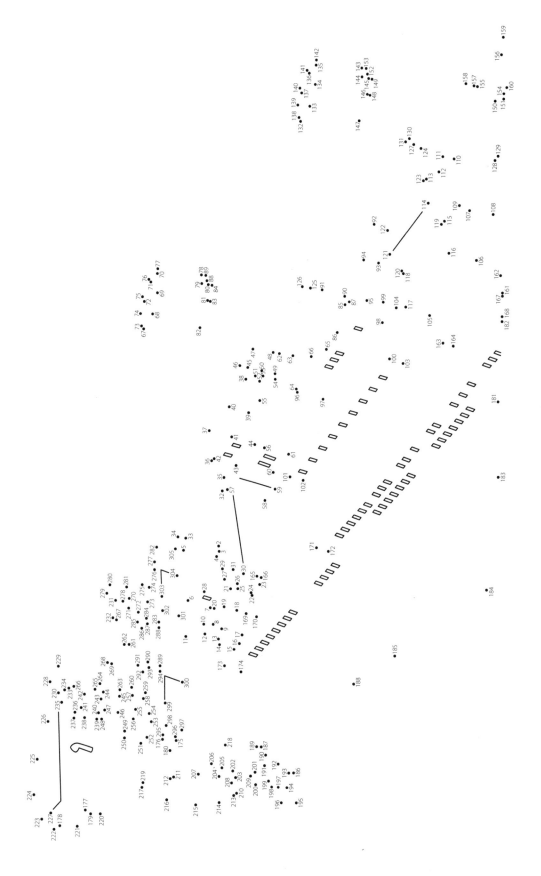

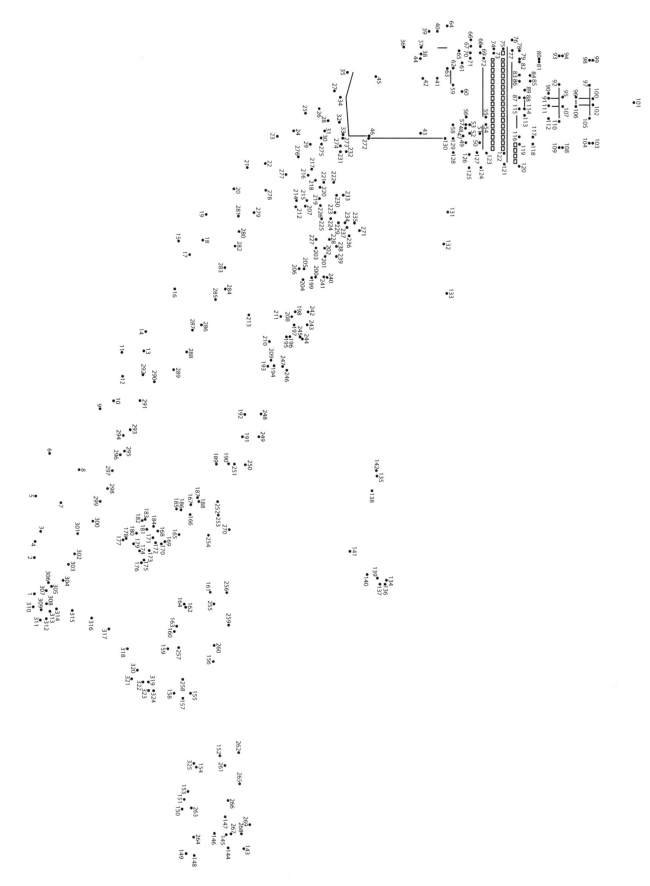

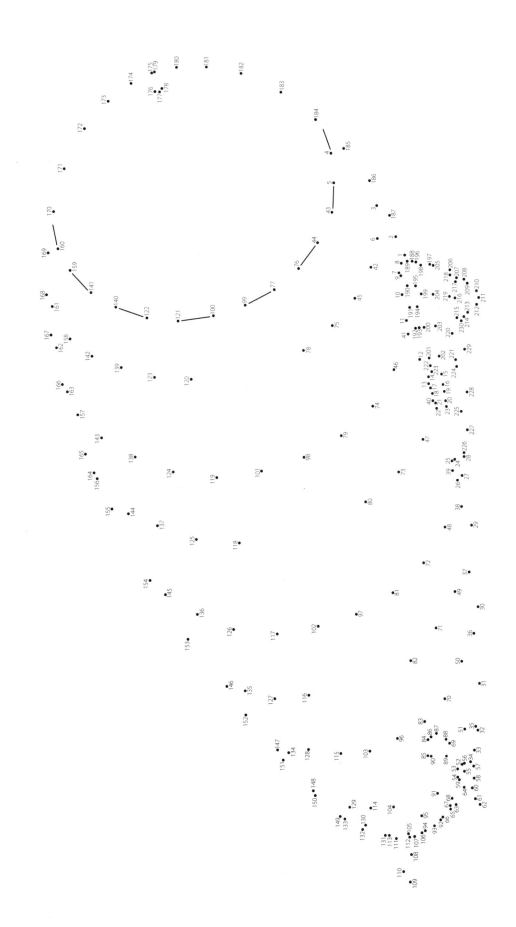

102

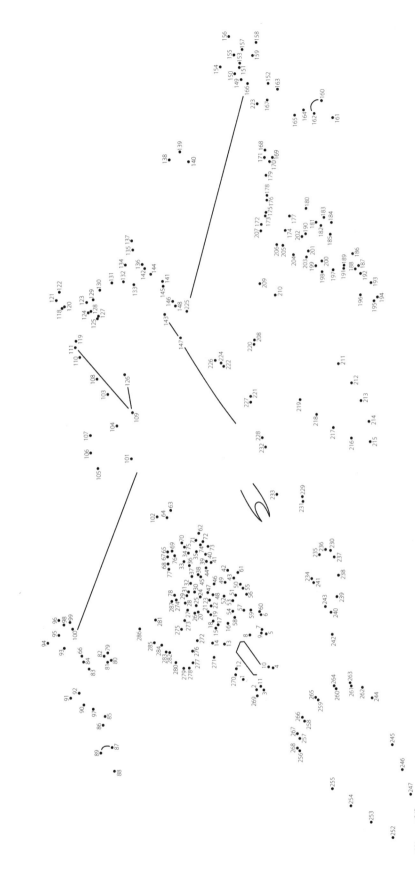

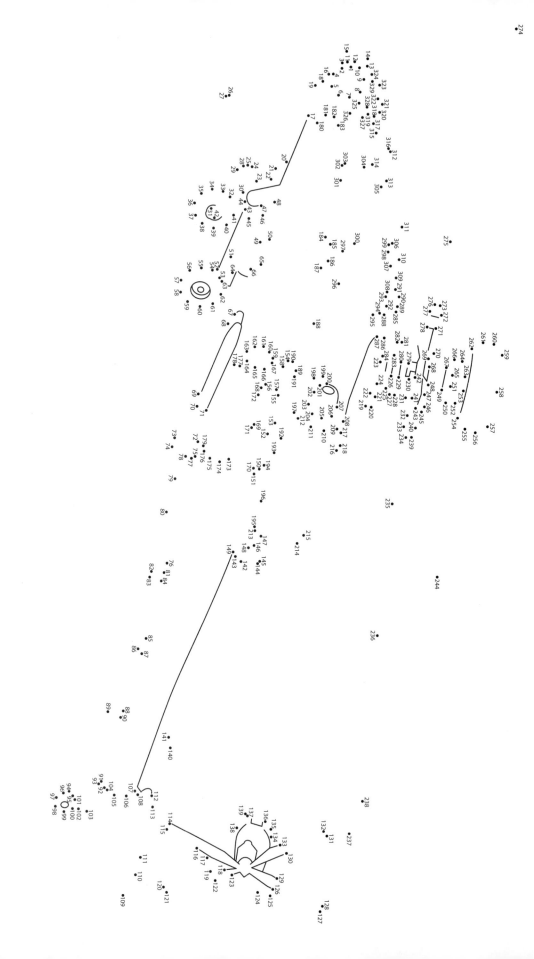

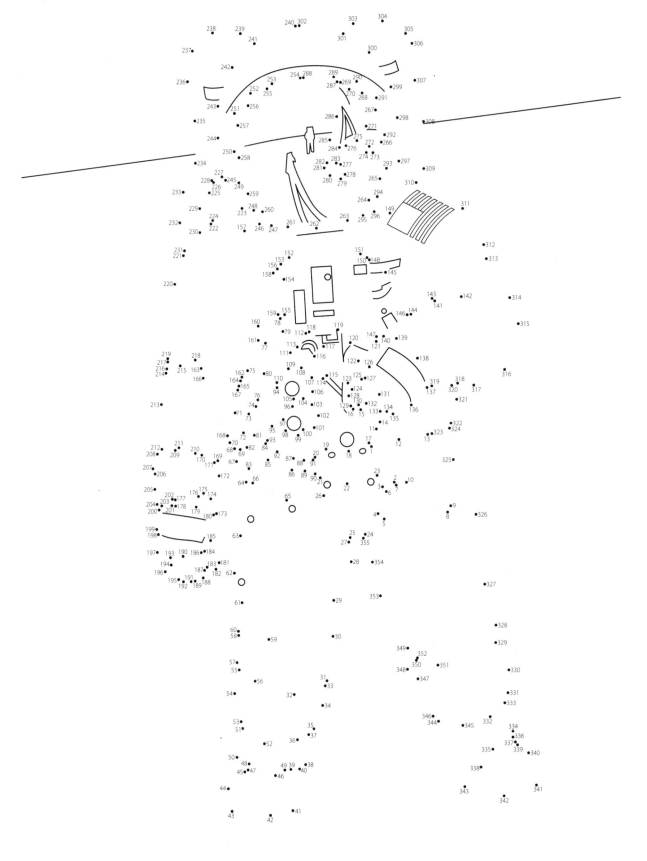

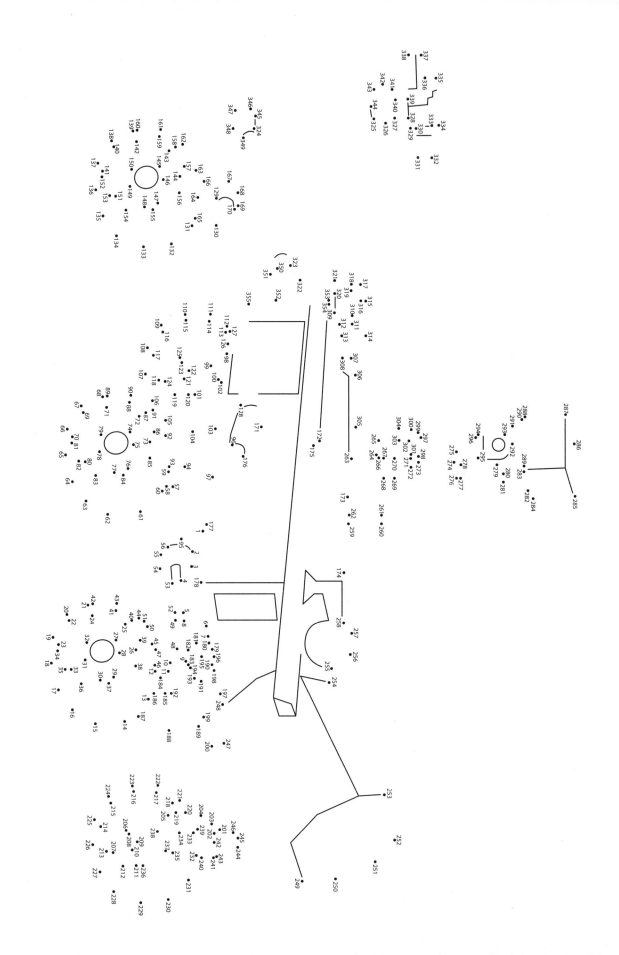

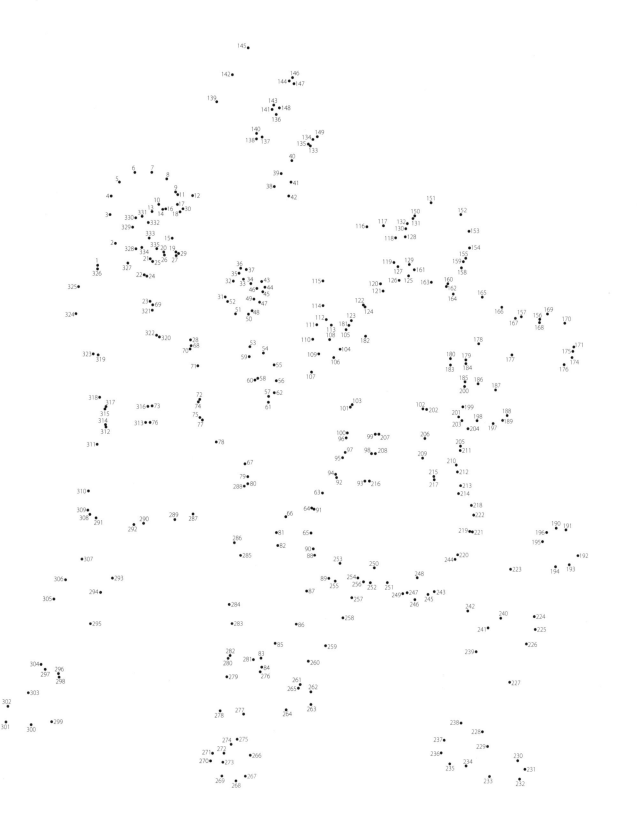

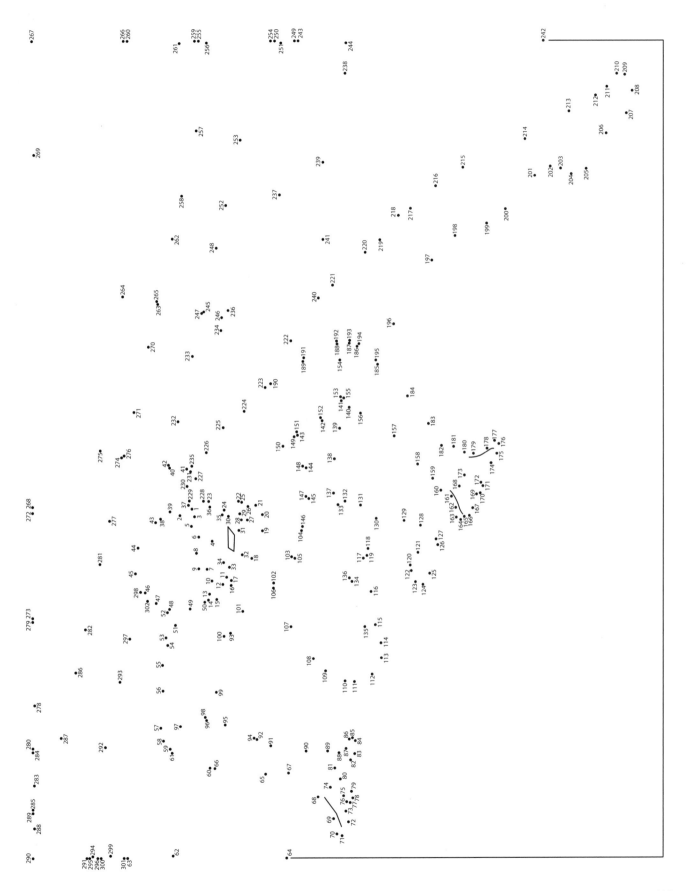

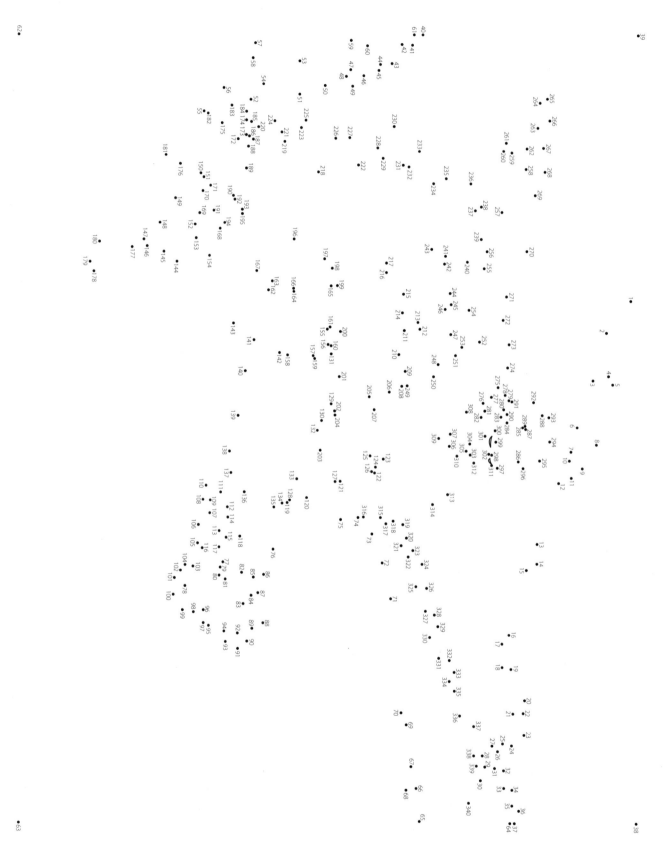

114

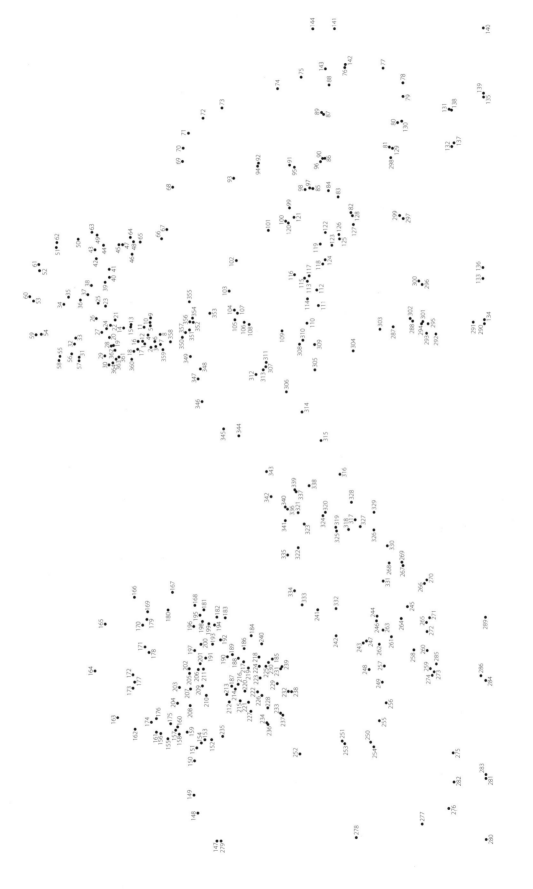

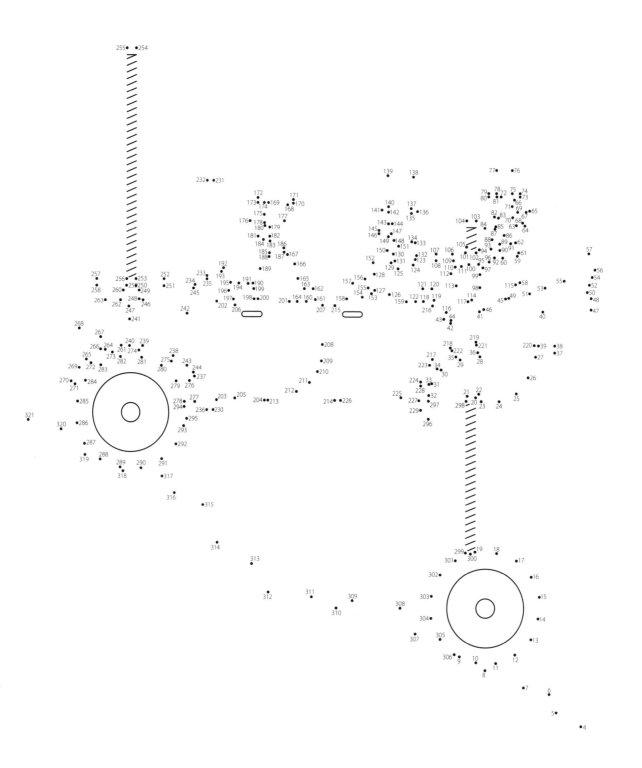

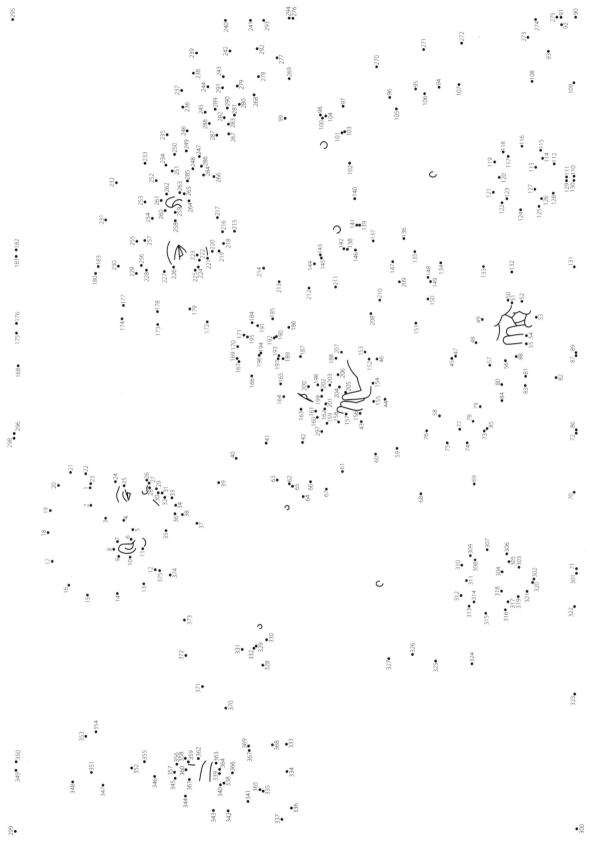

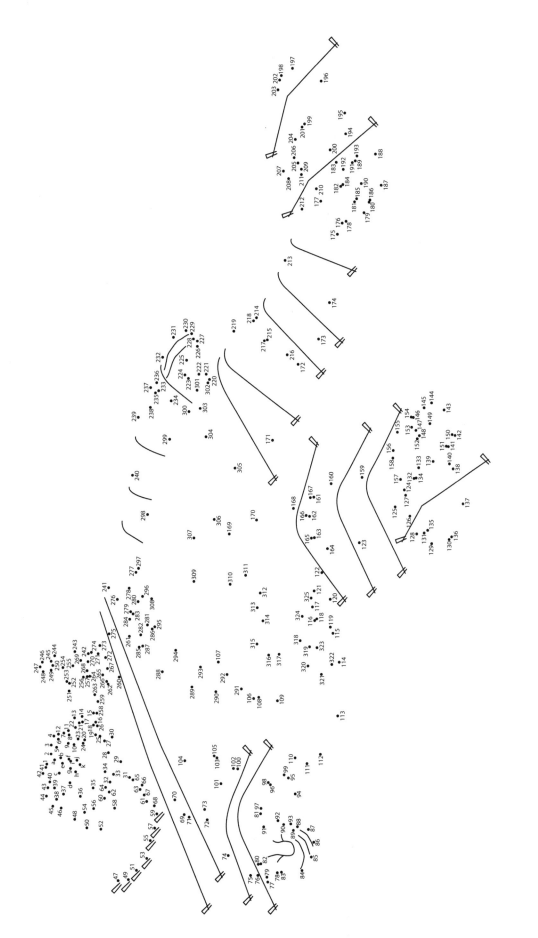

This picture is made from 2 continuous lines:
a) numbers and b) lower case letters

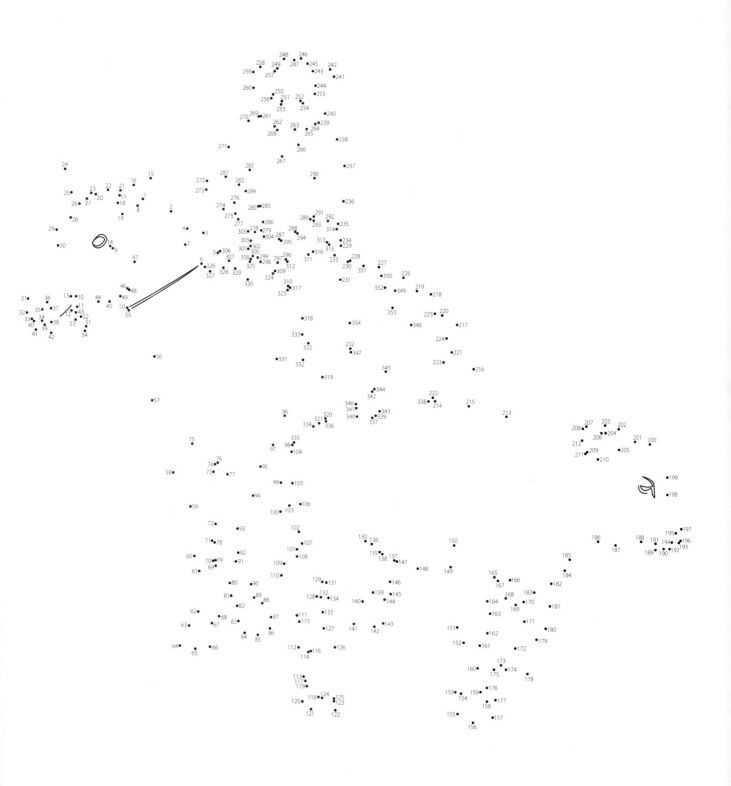

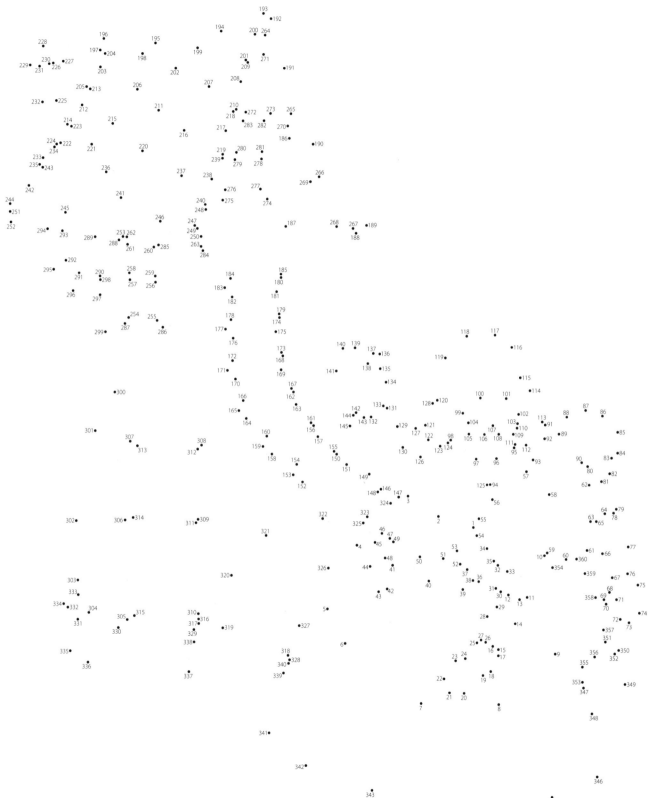

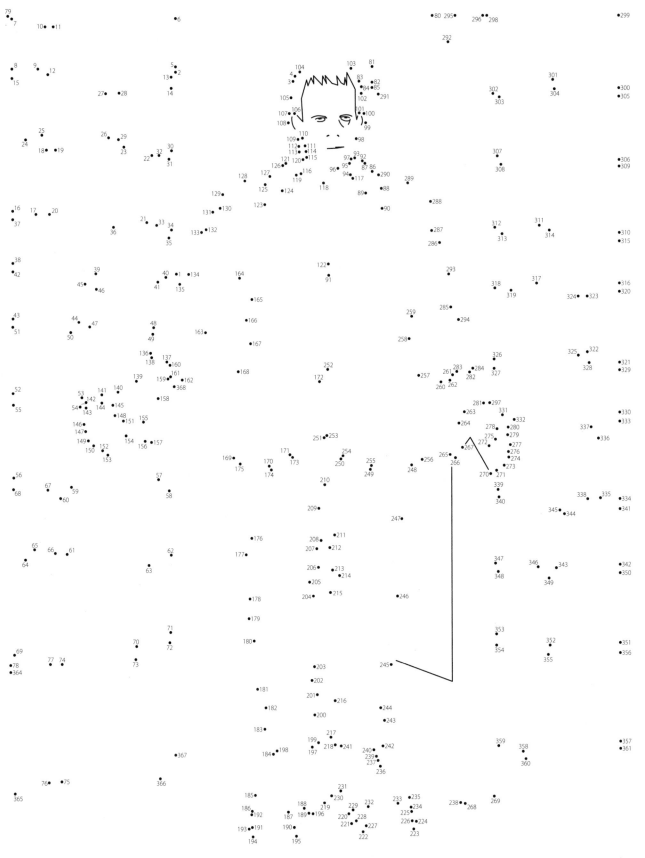

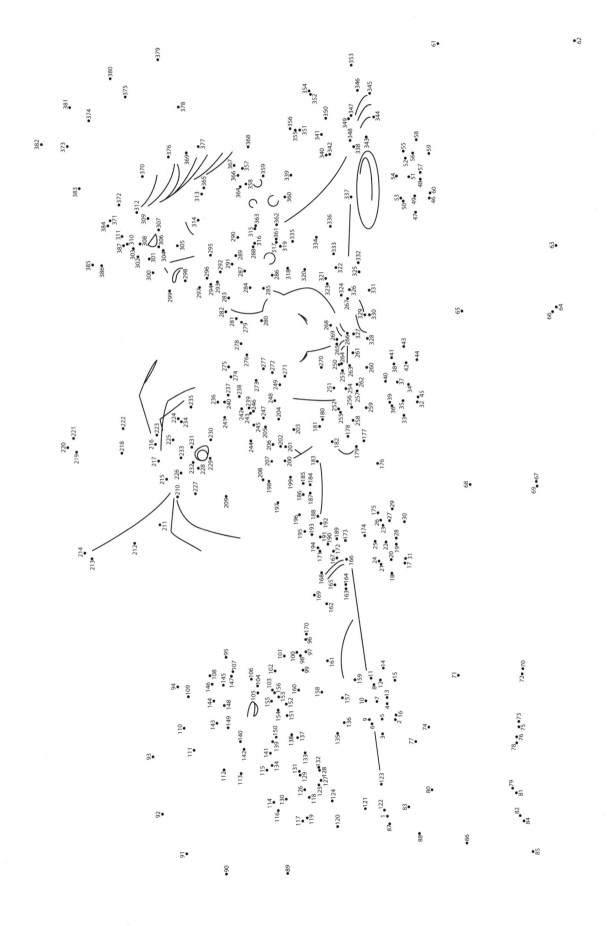

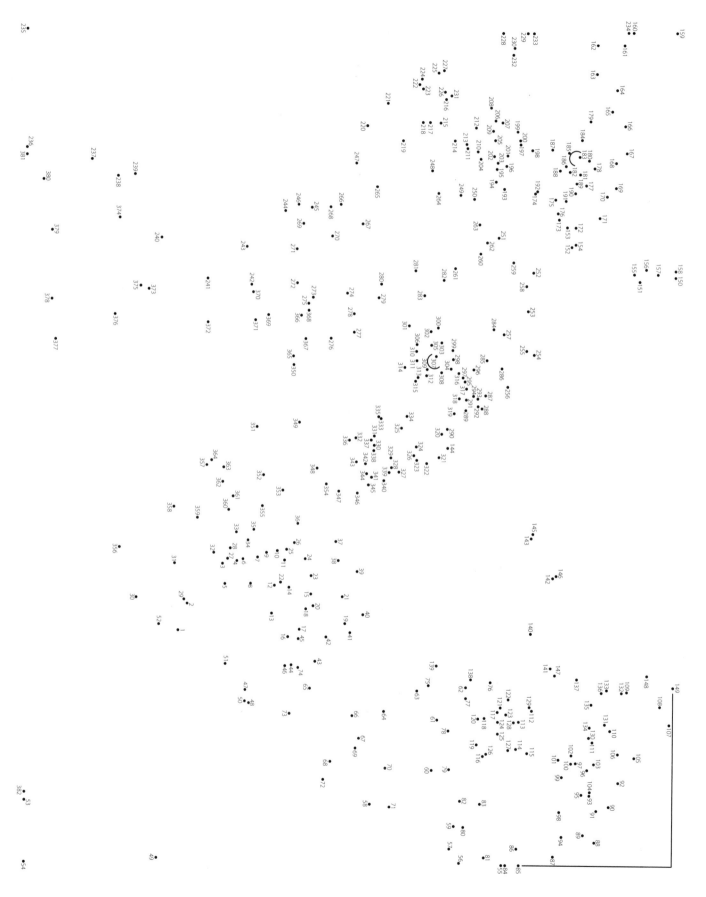

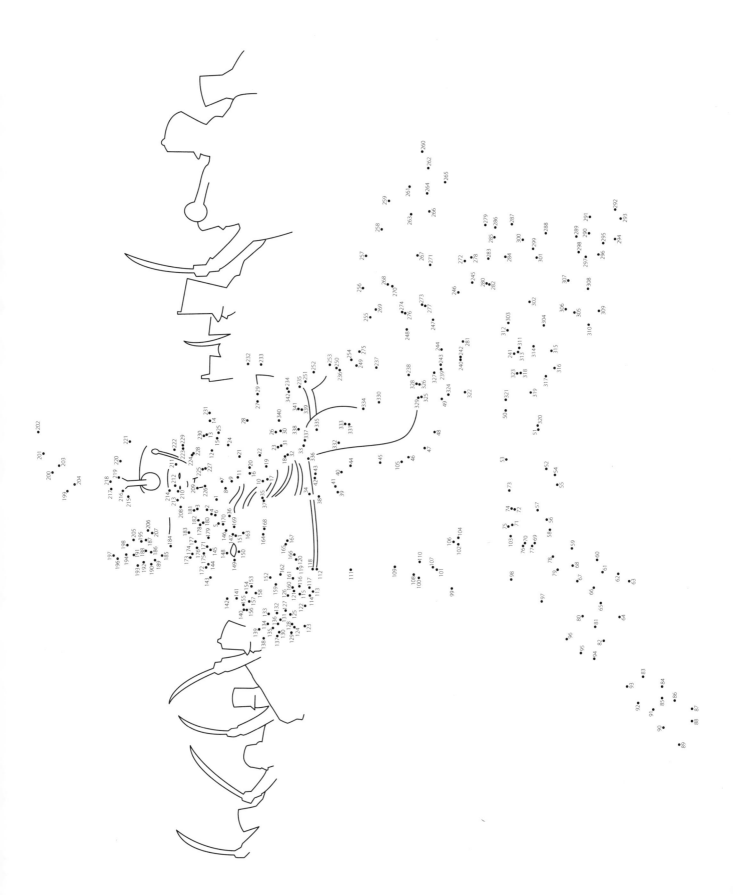

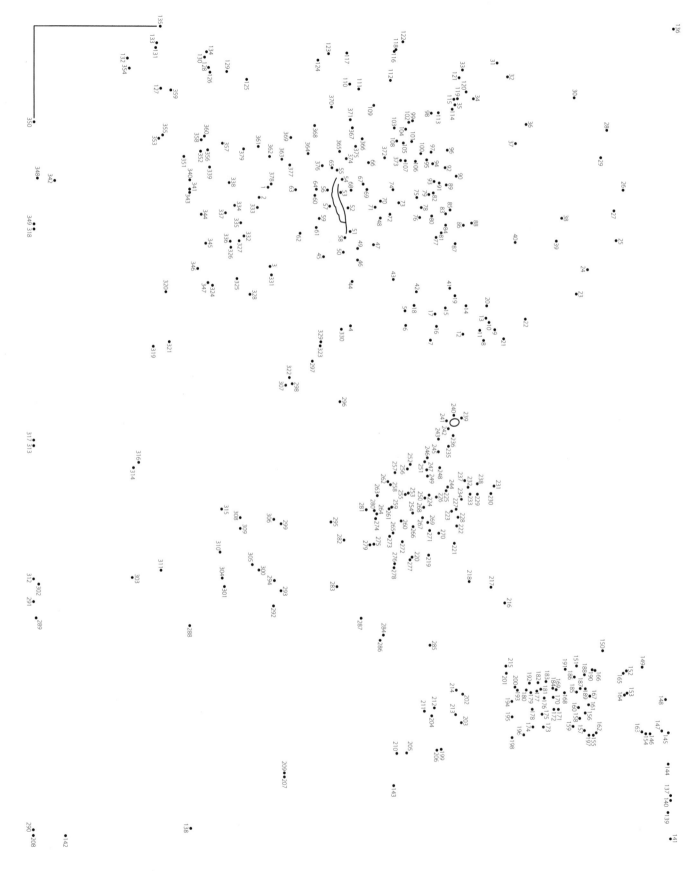

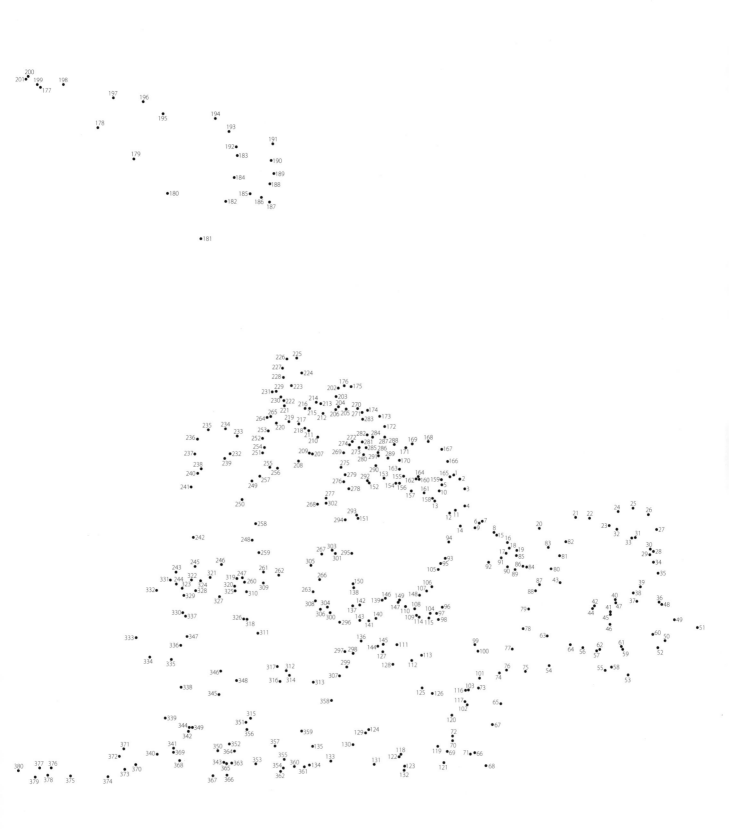

List of illustrations